LET'S LEAVE THE COUNTRY!

JACQUELINE JANNOTTA

LET'S LEAVE THE COUNTRY!
A GUIDE TO YOUR FAMILY YEAR ABROAD

LET'S LEAVE THE COUNTRY!
A Guide to Your Family Year Abroad

Copyright © 2019 Jacqueline Jannotta

Book cover design by designforwriters.com
Interior Artworks by Mattea Rothenberg, age 12

ISBN 978-0-9980381-0-0 (paperback)
ISBN 978-0-9980381-1-7 (ebook)

Library of Congress Control Number: 2018914645

Published by Becoming Better People Press
Portland, OR, USA
BecomingBetterPeople.us

This book is dedicated to
Nick, Chiara, and Mattea. You are my perennial magic…

CONTENTS

**Part Two: The Nuts and Bolts of Making Your
Dream Happen**

Part Three: Living the Dream

PREFACE

MY FAMILY'S YEARLONG ITALIAN ADVENTURE

"At least she's half-Italian," my grandmother proclaimed, referring to the woman who was to marry her only son. Never mind that my mother's half was northern Italian, it was still within the national borders and would be acceptable to the boisterous Abruzzese-Molisano clan she was marrying into. Hearing this as a child, I got the message loud and clear: "Watered-down Italian blood is still okay." And even louder: "Being Italian must be something worth holding on to."

Fast-forward a few decades, and here I am raising my half-Jewish daughters. They both bear my husband's surname, and their most celebrated link to their Italian heritage is a Christmas ravioli tradition. As a mother tasked with weaving the strands of family history into the next generation, what am I to do?

My girls relish the story of great-grandfather Ciro walking

1

all the way to France as a boy to catch a boat to America. And how he later went back to Italy to find a wife, before returning to Chicago so they could build their life together. They've also seen great-grandmother Mary's treasured letters from family in Liguria who anticipated her promised return. But as these ancestors retreat farther into the past, their stories fade and their essence becomes less tangible.

Sure, we can all sing the hymns of Frank Sinatra, or watch the occasional *Godfather* marathon. But I refuse to let my daughters' Italian-American identity diminish to a gesticulating stereotype born from a mythical land of meatballs and chianti. So, what better way to strengthen the Italian threads of their genetic tapestry than to move to *il bel paese* for a year!

After jumping through countless hoops to secure a visa and rent our house, we leaped across the same pond my ancestors did over a century ago. Our possessions: a few suitcases, a variety of Italian vocabulary words, and the names of ancestral villages spread across the Boot. Our landing spot: Genoa, Italy.

"Why Genoa?" The question followed us all over Italy. Genoa offered an ideal balance of urban and coastal, complete with a train station and airport. Its maze-like medieval beauty hid plenty of jewels for us to discover throughout our year—without the crowds of Florence or Rome. That a great-grandmother's hometown is nestled in nearby hills sealed the deal.

We enrolled our second- and fifth-grade girls in a local public school and proceeded to become the *americani*, attracting curious sidelong glances on a regular basis. Aside from a discernible exuberance, we blended right in—until we opened our mouths, that is. Our thick accents and bumbling speech gave us away every time.

While awaiting our *permesso di soggiorno* (the legal means to stay in Italy), we endured minor newbie struggles. We threw our hands up at using a bidet, but we pushed ourselves to master the assertive art of demanding the freshest focaccia behind the counter (hand gestures included!). We managed to deal with some grumpy vendors, but we also managed to make some friends. Yet on the much-anticipated day we earned our *permesso*, we still couldn't escape our odd outsider status. The *questura* officer puzzled, "Why on earth do you want to come here to our country, when so many of us want to go to your country?"

As we got into our Italian rhythm, we started to wonder the same thing. We had no problem getting used to the breathtaking views of the Mediterranean from the vertical city of Genoa. But trudging up its steep hills—and to our fifth-floor, no-elevator flat—left us a different kind of breathless. And, to be sure, we delighted in forgoing certain modern-day conveniences, such as owning a car. But hand-washing daily dishes or battling vertigo to hang laundry out our window—not so much.

Because ethnic food in Italy is in large part, well... Italian, we managed to suppress our cravings for other types of cuisine. We gave up on our beloved tacos after repeated attempts to re-create them using a local flat bread and mystery cheese. And one time, when we got our hands on a jar of bona fide peanut butter, we assembled the classic PB&J for the girls and their classmate. Our children devoured them with delight, while poor seven-year-old Emanuele politely tried to hide his horror as he choked down the *che schifo* mush.

Within a few months we learned the ropes in our new city. We could navigate public transportation (or not, if there was a strike!). We worked around the lengthy midday store closures and other inconveniences. But some obstacles proved more challenging. What would have been a simple task back home required a small army of friends contacting pharmacies in nearby countries so I could find a medicine for my daughter not sold in Italy. (Thank God for the Vatican drugstore!)

Despite our frustrations with our adopted homeland, we relished in its delights. We dove deep to understand regional foods. We learned the difference between *grana padana* cheese and *Par-*

migiano-Reggiano. We now get why *pesto genovese* actually tastes better with the rolled *trofie* as opposed to any ol' pasta shape.

Weekend trips thrilled to no end. Whether we sipped wine in Tuscany or drank in the stunning vistas of Sardinia or the Dolomites, Italy started to feel like home. Our toes tripped less over the centuries-old cobblestones beneath our feet, and our tongues started to trip less over the melodic Italian rolling Rs. It gave me envious joy that within only a few months my daughters had greater ease with Italian than I did, despite my decades of studying the language.

Touring iconic spots like Venice, Verona, or Pisa never disappointed, but they were hardly a match for our trips to ancestral towns. Because now we could actually converse with residents and forge a deeper connection with our family and its Italian origins. No longer would we be tourists passing through with an awkward smile and a camera. Instead, as descendants of those who left to seek out the American dream, we belonged in a different way.

For me, these visits stirred up the confusion of mixed identity. Ironically, I never felt more American than I did during our year in Italy. And in exploring the various branches and villages in my family tree, my Italianness actually became less clear. For despite its ancient past, Italy is a young country still defined by *localismo*. As a nation she is hard to pin down.

So to define the ethnic part of me, I was as much *genovese* or *bardigiana* as I was Italian. And my roots in Abruzzo and Molise barely reached beyond the precise hilltop villages that birthed my great-grandparents. Heck, if I figured in my father's DNA results, I could even consider myself a tiny bit Jewish. So, despite my grandmother's proclamations about being Italian, how definitively anything could I be?

My kids are even more patchwork than I am. And growing up in today's fluid and profoundly connected world means there's no predicting how they'll identify. But I already know that giving them this year in Italy has shaped them forever. Not only do they have another language, but they can view the world through another lens.

What else did our time in Italy give us? A year of being "outsiders" taught us what it's like to be an immigrant. Now can we feel a palpable empathy for immigrants today who struggle to become part of the American fabric, no matter where they're from. And walking in our ancestors' shoes gifted us a deeper sense for why they left their villages. It was as much to escape poverty as it was to forge a new way of life.

But most of all, today I understand at my deepest core the message I received as a young girl: There *is* something special about being Italian. Yet it has little to do with Italian blood. I now know why the country never stopped calling them.

Italy enchants.

Its spell endures generations and defies challenges. It's why food, music, and family lore alone can't tell the story. It's why we rearranged our lives for a yearlong adventure there. And it's why we'll keep going back for years to come.

A version of this essay was first published in the Winter 2018 issue of *Italian America*.

INTRODUCTION

COUNTLESS DELIGHTS FILLED OUR year in Italy. But plenty of harsh realities tormented us too. Such as the night before we moved to a new apartment when we discovered lice—and a broken water heater to boot. That head-chilling reality was hard to shake. Or, as mentioned in the Preface, that exhaustive hunt to track down a medicine for my daughter. In this book you'll hear a little more about our experience.[1] But this book is not about our delights or challenges, or even our adventure abroad. This book is about *your* adventure abroad, and how to turn *your* dream into a reality.

Creating our family year abroad didn't happen on a whim. At times it felt like tightrope walking in a wind tunnel. As we navigated the ins and outs of planning, friends would ask us how it was going. We replied with a lot of pat answers: "Fine"; "Still researching"; or "It's coming along." We remained unaware of their skepticism that we would actually pull it off. And we held our breath as we danced between determination and our *own* seeds of skepticism.

After we returned from Italy, those friends and countless others would quiz us on how we managed it, often with an eye toward how *they too* might manage something similar. It's because of them you're reading this book now. When someone asked me whether it's possible to "take a year off" and immerse in another part of the planet, I wanted to offer a thorough response. I wanted to be able to hand them a tangible guide and say, "Yes, it's possible."

WHAT TO EXPECT FROM THIS BOOK

Realizing your dream of living abroad for a year is like climbing a mountain. You'll face the mountain at certain points with no obvious trail ahead, and you'll wonder how the heck you're going to reach the summit. It will seem next to impossible. And why *would* you assume it to be possible? It's not part of the formula we've been sold about how life is "supposed" to go. We don't have a well-worn path to follow, but that doesn't mean we can't go there. It means we have to get comfortable forging a new path.

There are as many ways to do the year abroad as there are people who want to do it. Though uprooting for a time, and returning to life back home is daunting, it *is* doable. As you read, here's what to expect from *Let's Leave the Country!*:

- You'll get practical and emotional guidance on how to take yourself and your family abroad for a year, along with plenty of tips for planning a successful adventure—whether that's in the next several months or still in the someday realm.
- This book will help you navigate your options and weigh the pros and cons of each choice you'll make. It will also give you real examples of what others did, so you can try their choices on for size.

- While it won't tell you the GPS coordinates for your journey, this book *will* give you the figurative signposts in between your stops. You must fill out the rest with your details and dreams.
- *Let's Leave the Country!* offers a structure around which to plan, but leaves it up to you to find that sweet spot between spontaneity-squashing *over*planning and panic-inducing *under*planning.
- This book will help you manage the various challenges of daily life once you're abroad *and* upon your return. (Though you may end up taking the path of a few of the folks you'll encounter in these pages[2] who decided to adopt a permanent expat way of life.)

Each of the ten chapters details a guiding principle—summarized in the chapter title—that is key to a successful year abroad. The overarching strategy shared is based on my own experience, as well as the insights of others—all with the intention that you will follow your dream of living abroad instead of looking back someday, wishing you had.

WHAT EXACTLY ARE WE TALKING ABOUT?

In the seventeenth and eighteenth centuries, they called it the Grand Tour: Young aristocrats (mostly men, thanks to that unyielding patriarchy) would travel throughout Europe for a few years in order to gain a broad education and bring home lots of cool stuff. A more modest modern-day version of this is called the gap year.

The much-hyped gap year typically involves recent graduates, unencumbered by a job or family obligations, who travel the world before they hunker down and get "serious." But this book isn't about the grand tour or the gap year. Rather, it's about a calling so many of us have—that longing to see the world, or some special corner of it, in a deep and meaningful way.

I'm talking about a year abroad in which you cut yourself loose from all that you know in order to live a fresh, unpredictable life for a while. It's where you have an epic adventure before returning home to a new and improved version of yourself. And while it's called a *year* abroad, we need not be precise—though aiming for at least four seasons away is ideal.

The grand tour of 250 years ago belonged to the limited few born into the right families. Today, modern technology and transportation make it possible for just about anyone to work, transact, and travel to and from just about anywhere. The only barriers are time and money—big hurdles, to be sure. But more and more people are finding a way to follow this dream. And with some perseverance, out-of-the-box thinking, and a measure of faith that you'll land on your feet, you too can make such an adventure happen.

If you work in academia or for a company that offers the possibility of extended leave, your year abroad might look like a traditional sabbatical. Or maybe you can create your own version of a sabbatical by combining savings while shifting your work to be more virtual.

You might carve out eighteen months, like Tracey and Brian Carisch did, to homeschool the kids and lead a nomadic life while volunteering your way through the world. Or perhaps, like Bridget and Kevin Kresse, enough life events scream, "Do it now!" that you drag your three kids to a town in Tuscany, using your twelve months there to nourish creativity and reinvigorate your career upon return.

You could earn your teaching certificates, like Le Billington and her husband, Jon Joseph, did, and move to Kazakhstan for a year to teach English, then on to teaching stints in Indonesia, Turkey, and Zambia—with kids in tow. Or, like us, you could save for years to plunk down in Genoa where you hardly know a soul, because the thought of *not* doing it was more painful than all the effort it took to make it happen.

Throughout this book, you'll hear from these people and others, all with unique stories. And while each adventure takes a different shape, the road there follows a similar arc: We all start from the comfort zone we've grown accustomed to, extract ourselves from it, and arrive at our destination—even our "destiny"—to live abroad.

WHO IS THIS BOOK FOR?

Like us and the others whose adventures I share, you too dream of taking a year off to live in another part of the world. You long to travel and experience places in more than a passing-through-the-museum sort of way.

Perhaps you are somewhere midcareer, on the rise, or experiencing a plateau. Maybe you're trying to figure out what's next before your school-aged kids fly the coop. No matter the situation, the idea of jumping ship for a while entices you (even scares you), though it teeters on the impossible.

This book is mostly aimed at midcareer adults and their families. It's largely written for those who hope to design their own year abroad, independent of a company or institution. For those who plan to go abroad as a company employee, many of the practical challenges covered here will be a breeze, even though you may have more limited options of where to go or how you'll spend your time. Regardless of how you get abroad, the chapters in the book that focus on having a successful experience once there, as well as your transition back home, pertain to everyone.

And if the year abroad dream resonates with you, but you just aren't ready yet, this book is also for you. The "Save It for Someday" tips at the end of each chapter are written with you in mind. These suggestions allow you to take advantage of time and give yourself a leg up on planning your year abroad whenever you're ready to do it.

And last, while I will introduce some families who chose to travel throughout the world, this book primarily has the single-destination adventurer in mind. However, the pros and cons of traveling the world versus finding a new home for a year in a single locale will be explored in depth. No matter which type of adventure you choose, I trust you will gain valuable insight and guidance.

ℓℓℓ

Going abroad for a year is a tremendous undertaking, yet in my opinion, it's worth every ounce of sweat. The priceless gifts from our year in Italy continue to reveal themselves even several years after our return, and I suspect they will continue for decades to come. I wrote this book to offer inspiration, a light on the pathway to guide you—and the hand-holding I wish I had had when we embarked on our adventure.

A deeper motivation in writing this book stems from a fundamental belief I hold: We are here on Earth to evolve as a species and leave the planet better than we inherited it. To achieve that, it's essential to know other parts of the world more intimately—which leads us to diminish walls and build bridges across common ground.

Gaining perspective on global humanity is especially important for the next generation. To that end, I strive to give my kids a sense for the grand scale of their world—and the paradoxical truth that it's much smaller than they realize. Through our journey abroad, our girls learned to tap into strength and intelligence they didn't know they had, and they learned that obstacles can be overcome.

I believe if more people experienced a year abroad, only good can come of it. My hope is that this book will play a small part in helping to broaden our collective horizon.

Part One: Bringing the Dream to Life

CHAPTER ONE

BUILD THE BRIDGE FROM FANTASY TO REALITY

OVER THE COURSE OF my adult life I've quizzed people at random on *the* "thing" they might be missing, their biggest life fantasy. One answer that persists across the board is, "Someday I want to live in another country." (In case you're wondering, a distant second in my unscientific poll is "to live in a self-designed community with my closest friends.") Before we can ponder how to answer that question, our dreams are eclipsed by family, friends, weekend tasks, an occasional vacation, a developing career, a mortgage, and so on.

That was the case with me. When I first traveled to Europe as a twenty-year-old with my dad, the seeds of a dream were planted. But after college graduation I focused on getting a job and building a career. When the desire tugged again, my meager bank account kept my belief system hostage. I didn't even try. Then marriage, a move, and a growing family pushed the dream aside—until it reared its tantalizing head again.

When you have a live-in-another-country fantasy, the easiest response is to keep it as a "someday" dream, as in, maybe *someday* you'll get to it. And if it never becomes a priority, it probably stays in that fantasy realm forever. Maybe that's okay. Certainly, some things are better left as fantasies. But if the fantasy taunts you, goading you to turn your dream into reality, there are things you can do today to start the process.

In this chapter we examine the essence of your dream and begin to shape the tangible goal of living abroad. And though the goal will morph as you explore various pathways to get yourself overseas, adequate definition should enable you to see the next best steps in front of you. Just like life, you won't be able to control everything that comes your way. But taking these first steps to define your dream gives you something you can start to sculpt into reality.

GRASPING AT THE YEAR ABROAD FANTASY

You may already hold a clear picture of what your year abroad looks like. Perhaps you see yourself in New Zealand, traversing exotic terrain, and exploring a different beach every weekend. Or maybe you picture yourself exchanging "*Bom Dia*" as you pass smiling Portuguese villagers on the sunny cobblestoned lane that leads to your kids' school. Or your yearning to give back has you imagining a service adventure for your family, volunteering with kids in Cambodia. The scenarios are infinite. If this is you, great. Read on and give your dream more definition.

For many of us, however, it's the mere notion of wanting to live abroad that teases us. The where and the details are less significant than the journey and experience it represents. We can sense the thrill of living in an unexplored land. We can taste the freshness of an undiscovered palate, even though we don't know what aspect of the olfactory gland it will tickle. All we know is that we long for something markedly different from the noises and vistas of our current daily routine.

We often suppress our pangs for this enticing "other" life because they are too vague. Or because a voice in our head calls out, "Don't rock the boat!" or "Unknown danger ahead!" Usually the volume is high enough to drown out the whisper of "Seize the day!" We're stuck in a battle of inner voices that prevents us from even considering such an adventure.

OBSTACLES, ANYONE?

Before we dig into defining the year abroad fantasy, chances are the phrase "Yeah, but…" nags in the background of your thoughts. The "but" can be anything—your job, family, career trajectory, the state of the world. More often than not it's about money.

While such hurdles may be real, put them aside for now. Instead, begin to define what your living abroad dream would look like—even if it's just pie in the sky right now. This is an essential step before you can address potential obstacles.

Robert Kiyosaki, the author of *Rich Dad Poor Dad*, tells the story of growing up poor, and how his father would react when faced with an added expense. If it was perceived as a luxury, his dad would always say, "We can't afford it." Not wanting to replicate his father's scarcity mentality, the author learned to mimic what his wealthier friends' fathers said: "How *can* we afford it?"

It's a simple mindset shift I urge you to adopt:

- Instead of saying, "I can't leave my job for a year," ask yourself, "How can I leave my job for a year?"
- Instead of thinking you can't lose traction in your career trajectory, think about how this could fuel your personal life trajectory, including your career.

- Instead of assuming your kids are too young/old, commit to exploring how a year abroad plan can fit for their particular age.
- Instead of letting concerns about aging parents stop you from your dream, ask yourself how you can still be of support while away for a year.
- Instead of allowing scary global events to keep you from considering a year abroad, own the fact that you'll make wise choices amidst a world you can't control.

Shifting to such a mindset doesn't happen naturally. The cynical side of you wants to focus on the obstacle because it's easier to stay stuck than it is to devise a solution.

Upending a "stay put" mentality was probably the single most significant hurdle that stood in the way of my family's year in Italy.

"I don't know that we'll be able to pull this off," I would say to my husband.

"What's to stop us?" Nick would counter.

Every time I'd bring up an issue that would get in the way of going, he'd point to a potential workaround. After a while, I began to see how my default thinking kept me stuck. I learned to remind myself it's in my power to shift toward a more open mindset. The pep talks I gave myself started to sink in.

With self pep talks and a little effort, you too can get in the habit of swatting away the "Yeah, but…" thoughts like annoying flies. My hope is that you'll stay open while you read this book, so you can start seeing alternate routes where roadblocks stood before. Because once you take the step of truly defining your dream, then you can carve out a path toward it. Obstacles may still be there—and they ultimately may shift the timing or shape of your goal to live abroad. But you will be in control of managing those hurdles instead of the hurdles determining your life plans.

GO PIE IN THE SKY

So, putting the notion of obstacles aside, let's go pie in the sky.

To cross this bridge from fantasy to overseas reality, you'll want to uncover what it is about the dream of living abroad that inspires you. The following questions touch upon several aspects of daily life that dominate a typical human experience. Their purpose is to jostle your imagination and help you clarify the goal of doing a year abroad.

As you ponder these questions, find a way to record your answers. If you like to journal, write down your responses. If you're more visual, cut out images from magazines and create a vision board. If daydreaming is what you do best, then focus hard on your answers and sear them in your mind so they become more than a passing flurry of thoughts.

The goal is to create specifics, but without any rigid expectations. You need to get a sense for what your vision is—even if some of the answers bring you to the edge of your comfort zone. And even if some of those answers seem to contradict one another. Think of this exercise as the Location setting being activated on a mobile device: Accuracy varies, but the more coordinates you give it, the better aim it has.

As you read over the following questions, picture yourself in various scenarios of a potential year abroad experience, and let them spark further questions. Again, don't consider any roadblocks, just focus on desire: what inspires you, what lights you up.

Your Daily Surroundings

- Do you picture yourself surrounded by nature, in the countryside? Does the scent of falling leaves, blooming flowers, or ocean mist call to you?
- Or do you get more energy from a faster urban pace, where the bustle of people along vibrant city streets dominates the scene?

- Perhaps it's something in between: a village that hums with a couple of cafés and markets, surrounded by countryside?
- As far as the land itself, do you envision hills, mountains, or a particular terrain? Or is the picture incomplete without a body of water nearby?
- Do you care about climate? Are you most alive with heat and humidity? Or does chilly and cozy bring out the best in you?
- What about seasons? Do you need all four? Or would you like to experience life closer to the equator, which offers an endless summer? Or maybe you're intrigued by the midnight sun and unintimidated by a dark sky throughout winter?

The Rhythm of Your Days

- Even if you might work during part of your year abroad, when you ponder your free time, do you see yourself being more physically active or more intellectually active?
- Do you visualize yourself in a creative pursuit, such as photography, painting, or drawing? Making something? Writing?
- Are you anticipating a year of feeding your curiosity by taking classes, studying a language, or some other form of intellectual challenge? Maybe you can't wait to devour a long list of books you've been too busy to enjoy?
- Do you see yourself interacting with people in some type of volunteer effort, or even teaching locals your language?
- Does physical activity get your juices flowing, such as hiking, biking, camping, or climbing?
- Or do you respond to the call of cultural activity— theater, art, music, museums?

- Do you imagine a nomadic year in travel mode, perpetually navigating your surroundings?
- What else comes to mind when you think about your daily activity during a possible yearlong sabbatical?

What Feeds You and Fits You

- Are there any foods you never tire of? What would you welcome an endless supply of—fish? Fresh vegetables? Exotic fruit? Pasta? Rice dishes? Cheeses? Wine? Beer?
- Are you an omnivore with a very curious palate, or do you tend to be a picky eater? Does your palate prefer spicy or simple?
- Do you follow a religion or philosophy that requires a certain set of foods or customs? If so, will these customs be challenging to maintain in various parts of the globe?
- As for your appearance, do you prefer to blend in based on how you look and dress? Or will you be okay standing out, either ethnically or by your clothing?
- Is there a particular culture that calls you?
- Besides the ubiquitous background of American pop music that can be heard around the world, if your ears were regularly met with a radically different sound, would that entice you or unnerve you?
- If you lived in a country with a dominant religion that is not your own, would you find it exotic and enchanting or constantly chafing?

Connecting with Other People

- Do you speak more than one language?
- Do you want to learn another language, but for whatever reason have never gotten around to it?

- Are you a communicative person regardless of language? If not, how *do* you best interact with people?
- Does the thought of stumbling through a conversation in a foreign language fill you with dread? Or does it offer a *thrill* akin to diving out of a plane?
- When you envision yourself with whomever joins you abroad, what simple scenarios bring a smile to your face?

Question Yourself from Another Angle

If you think of your responses to the questions thus far as kindling, hopefully it's crackling a bit. The aim is for images to form, and for desire to awaken. If so, keep pondering to see if anything else bubbles up. If you still have trouble drumming up specifics about your year abroad, then let's come at it from a different angle.

Perhaps you're the type of person who has an easier time reacting *against* something. If that's the case, examine the things in your life that are pushing you toward a year abroad, so you can start to paint a clearer picture of a dream that calls you. See if you can discern themes and patterns that form when you answer the following questions. Then revisit the previous questions and try to gain more clarity.

Reflect on where you are now in your life:

- What isn't working for you in your daily routine that you would like to change? Are you happy with your career path, or do you feel pulled in another direction? Are you in control of your daily rhythms, or are they controlling you?
- Do you feel the need to shake things up? If so, can you intuit what aspect of your life feels stuck?
- What is it about your current city or town that has you thinking some other part of the planet would fulfill what's missing? Is it largely an aesthetic thing? Or a deeper cultural flaw you don't believe exists in another country?

- Are your friendships and other relationships fulfilling? Is there some way that living abroad for a while might enliven them—or offer you a clean slate?
- Is there some part of this dream that has you fantasizing about a more permanent move abroad? If so, what aspects of your current life would you absolutely *not* want to give up? If you can picture yourself switching things up to live abroad, what can you picture doing for work? In that scenario do you see yourself getting by and living a simple life, or do you see yourself in a job similar to the one you have now? Or is it some unknown in between?

Take a Wider Angle

When you have the beginnings of a vision—even if it's hazy— throw these questions into the mix:

- What are you curious to learn more about that you can't access from where you are?
- If this adventure includes your kids, what would you like them to get out of going abroad for a year? A new language? A different understanding of the world? If so, what aspect of the world? How about a different understanding of themselves? What aspect would serve them well?
- When thinking about nurturing your family relationships, what kind of time away together do you envision?
- And zooming out, is there any bigger picture, bigger personal mission deep inside, that you might bring forth by tearing yourself away from your routine and gaining a wider perspective?

THE NON-VACATION PLAN

The aim here is not necessarily to have detailed answers for each question, or to figure out the exact coordinates of your beautiful spot abroad. Rather, you should get a sense of what is drawing you *to* that beautiful place. By picturing yourself living abroad and understanding the motivations behind your dream, you'll start to distinguish this from simply a yearlong vacation. Because it won't be a vacation in any traditional sense of the word.

While there are many savvy explorers reading this who regularly aim for deep experiential travel, for many people vacations can be described as "zoo travel." This is where you travel to a new place, meander, window shop, tour museums, read pamphlets, eat food, ooh and aah, and sleep in new places. If you're lucky, someone will invite you to take part in a cultural activity. Bonus if you manage to strike up an insightful conversation with a local. But, by and large, meaningful interaction with residents is minimal.

Over the course of your vacation you might assess why home is better, or why the grass is greener. And within a couple of weeks you head back to your familiar rhythm. The experience fades into the background of your life, apart from the photographs you'll pull out on occasion to remind you of the zoo-like experience you had.

If you're reading this book, you probably aren't after a year of zoo travel. You're dreaming of something else, something much deeper and more rewarding, something that will resonate with you and your family for years, that could inform and influence you for the rest of your lives. If this describes you, then your next step is to home in on what will propel the dream forward and actually aid you in making it happen.

FUEL YOUR YEAR ABROAD PLAN WITH A WHY

If you've ever taken part in formulating a mission statement for a group or organization, then you realize the amount of energy and patience it takes to get it right. And even then it's never clear whether the mission statement has real integrity or is more of a big compromise so everyone can go home. That's why the simplicity of Simon Sinek's TED Talk[3] resonates with so many people. The author and thought leader distills the reason for success—personal or organizational—down to a simple question: *Why?* Why are you doing what you're doing?

You can certainly get yourself abroad if you don't answer this question. But in terms of having a smoother path to getting there, and a deeper experience once there, answering it will pay big dividends. And when you're doing this as a family, it's best to be on a similar page with your Why. Knowing your Why fuels a successful experience.

And while you may not have a literal mission statement, when the umpteenth person asks you why on earth you want to pull your kids out of school, or take a detour from your career path, trust me when I tell you: You will want to give them a rock-solid answer, if only to preserve your mental energy from the litany of questions you're going to face.

So, if someone—or you yourself—were to ask you right now why you want to live abroad, how would you respond? The answers I usually hear off the bat are things like:

- We want to expand our horizons.
- We want our children to be citizens of the world.
- We want to see the world while we're young.
- We've always wanted to live in another country.
- We want to gain a broader perspective.

These may all be true and valid reasons to uproot your life to live in another country. But I encourage you to dig deeper and make your reason more personal. Your Why should be something that makes your heart sing. When you express it, you should light up inside.

Your reason shouldn't be a negative one having to do with escape, such as not liking your job, your town, your home, and/or your social life. These negative things can *inform* your Why, but they in themselves are not powerful enough to keep you going. Wanting your kid to escape middle school, for example, does not mean that moving abroad will make for a rosy passage through adolescence.

It's a safe bet that if you're trying to escape something unhappy in your current life, you will likely create another unhappy situation wherever you land. You need a reason that is not about running *away* from something but rather is about pulling you *toward* something more fulfilling.

Your personal motivation, your goal for going abroad, should ideally be something that is achievable. For example, when we set out for Italy, my internal motivation was to forge a deeper relationship with the culture of my ancestors and for my kids to have a second language. It's personal. It connects to something deep that moves me. And no matter how the chips would fall, or what challenges we would encounter, my experiences would contribute to my relationship with the culture and language.

Italian bureaucracy is just one of the challenges we encountered. I did *not* like all the official hoops we had to jump through to obtain our *permesso di soggiorno*. Yet, every single annoying bureaucratic encounter got me deeper into the language and culture and built my relationship to it. Moving to Italy for a year, coupled with putting my kids in the local public school as opposed to an international one, meant that achieving my essential goals—my Why—was a foregone conclusion.

My husband, on the other hand, simply craved a sabbatical. He longed for time and space to rethink his career, find a new perspective, even work on a book. Little did we know that our kids would be in school a mere five hours a day until lunchtime, which we made at home.

Our few free morning hours would largely be filled with hand-washing dishes, hanging laundry, and shopping for the day's meals before the markets closed for *siesta*. The extra time left over for us to tap into the inspiration of Italy's creative masters? Those moments were spent climbing up and down the stairs to our fifth-floor apartment.

This is not to say my husband had an unfulfilling year. Rather, he had to adjust his expectations and make a dramatic shift on what he aimed to gain from the year—because he couldn't shift the reality of life in Italy.

His book writing became catch-as-catch-can "note taking." Deep reflection on a career change became simple reflection on life. Rich creative exploration became daily exploration of a new corner of the world. While this still made for a rich experience for my husband, developing his Why at a deeper level might have made for a smoother adjustment and more moments of joy.

I too envisioned writing a book, but if my Why had been to finally get away to write the novel of my dreams, I would have crashed, burned, and failed. I would have been making the assumptions that:

a) I'd have huge luxurious swaths of time (with two school-aged kids—impossible!); and

b) that I'd have the mental calm and stability to write with depth (while grappling with a second language, setting up a home, trying to find community? Ha!).

Your Whys will be deeply personal, and it will serve you well to know what they are. Bridget and Kevin Kresse, of Little Rock, Arkansas, had tragically lost a couple of people dear to them. This was a wake-up call to make their year abroad dream happen. So in September 2010, they moved to Lucca, a small town in Tuscany, where Kevin would replenish his inspiration as an artist. *Carpe diem* became the rocket fuel that propelled them onward.

For many of us, watching kids race through childhood, or the simple hurtling toward middle age or later, is enough of a motivator to get us going. But even then, aim for something deep and personal. Like George Mason and Salli Slaughter, who ventured around the world with their two kids in the 1990s. They wished "to see the world and not be afraid of it"—a simple yet powerful directive.

If you and your brood are not all on the same page, find ways to align. Laura Wall Mansfield knew a yearlong family trek around the globe was in the cards way before she had a family. In fact, it was part of an agreement she made with her husband when they got engaged. Fast-forward to 2016 and two kids later as they embark on the year of *her* dreams. But what about everyone else in the family?

Her husband, a tennis fanatic, and her twelve-year-old, a sports junkie, will each explore their passion as they travel the globe. With the help of their personal network—both existing and sought out (more on that in Chapter 4)—they set up a soccer-playing experience in Germany as well as baseball in Cuba for her tween. Her husband will look forward to world-class tennis tournaments in various destinations around the globe—in the flesh, instead of in front of his television. And their nine-year-old son, a budding foodie, will educate his palate in a way that most North American chefs only dream about. (Peruse travelingsons. com to learn how the Mansfield family's intentions transpired.) The pursuit of these passions will encompass the Whys that keep them going.

Whatever your deepest reason, know it and know it well. There may be several elements that comprise your Why, but figure out what resonates at your deepest core. This will be your touchstone when things get difficult—not only as you plan your year abroad but as you experience it.

Again, this is not to say you can't make the year abroad happen on a wing and a prayer, without a focused motivation. But owning that Why will offer more horsepower as you cross the bridge from fantasy to reality. And sometimes that added oomph is just what you need to get across.

CROSSING THE BRIDGE

Whatever your circumstances, and whatever resources you bring to this endeavor of living abroad, you are starting from a good place. If you are finding the time and inclination to read this book, you are educated and at least somewhat tech-savvy, and you hold the mental space to consider a major leap like a year abroad. A significant portion of people on the planet don't have such privileges.

Ironically, this kind of abundance in your life might even be your Achilles' heel. You may delight in *so much* shiny goodness that the idea of breaking away from your comfortable rhythm terrifies you. This pull to stay on track might be deemed your personalized golden handcuffs. And staying put might be a valid "should." Only you can discern whether you're embracing the truth about bad timing or a wrong choice or succumbing to the seduction of a high-comfort zone.

How and when will you know you're ready to embrace your dream of creating a year abroad? Well, the short answer is: *When you have a vision of your year abroad, and why you want to do it.* Because when you have a handle on what you're seeking and why you're seeking it, that's when the fog dissipates, allowing you to see the bridge ahead. Your clarity brings it out of hiding.

In the coming chapters, we'll get into the practical steps involved in *crossing* that bridge. But first, know this: As you are in the process of realizing your goal, you will feel deflated at times. Plenty of times. You'll wonder if it's worth the effort, whether you can hack all the uncertainty while keeping your sanity intact. Those moments are your prompt to take a deep breath and return to your Why. At any point you need a nudge, ask yourself like I did: On my deathbed, if I reflect on my biggest fulfillments and my biggest regrets, will my year abroad fall under the former category or the latter?

I did not want my dream of living abroad to fall under the regret column, so I refused to let it wither into a "shoulda woulda coulda." What will you do?

eelee

SAVE IT FOR SOMEDAY TIPS

- Start tuning in to the small voice inside you that wants to live abroad. Keep a browser open in your current life to act as a window on your Why. Ask yourself what might feed you at a deeper level. This way, you'll have a well-developed divining rod when it comes time to define your deepest reasons for taking a year abroad.
- Create and build a file to keep notes on your fantasy year abroad. Include images that resonate with you, articles that strike you, musings that entice you. This could also be an electronic notebook, an app such as Evernote, or even a Pinterest board. Seek to fuel the dream, so when the time is right in your life, you're ready to go.

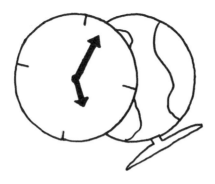

CHAPTER TWO

GENTLY PUT YOUR DREAM ON THE SPACE-TIME CONTINUUM

By now you hold a more focused vision of what your year abroad might look like. Your next step is to take aspects of the nebulous fantasies from the exercises in the last chapter and give them substance. Start by pinning down major things onto the reality-based space-time continuum. To put it more precisely, figure out the *where* (space) and the *when* (time).

Maybe you already have a strong sense of where you want to live for the year, and all you need to do is pinpoint the specific city or town (no small task, I might add). Or perhaps you see the world as your oyster while you consider several locations to meander through over the months. These adventures are distinctly different experiences, each of which we'll explore.

Then there's your when. Are you going a year from now? Three years from now? And for how long? This book focuses on the *year* abroad because I believe there's value in experiencing all four seasons and completing a full scholastic term if you have school-aged kids.

When you stay pulled out of your previous rhythm long enough, you get a real feel for a different place—*and* a different pace. Plenty of former expats will say that two years or more is necessary for a rich experience, so twelve months is a subjective measure. Yet even if you manage to only swing five months away from home, that's far better than the standard two-week vacation. The specifics need not be set in stone at this point. But to form a plan, you must zero in on the where and when.

'ROUND THE WORLD, OR ONE SPECIAL PLACE?

As you prepare to join the exclusive but growing club of people who upend their lives for a period of expat adventure, know that you'll fall into one of two camps:

- The see-the-world folks, or
- The immerse-in-a-single-culture gang.

These are markedly different experiences, each one sacrificing a great deal as well as offering a great deal. Although both follow much of the same trajectory in regards to planning, I've charted out the major distinctions to help you make and own a clear choice.

'ROUND THE WORLD	ONE SPECIAL PLACE
Constant travel means you'll see a wide variety of places for a shorter time, allowing you to avoid the darker side of a culture. Limited time might also keep you from developing strong relationships in any single place.	Making a home for a year in a single place allows you to integrate into the community, build friendships, and really get to know the good *and* bad of a single culture, which might feel confining.
The repeated packing up and moving on after a few weeks can be a thrill, but it also might sap your energy.	Getting settled allows you to create a way to recharge regularly. Any travel you do will always bring you back to a familiar home base.
When bringing kids, going around the world involves homeschooling in some form—without the complications (or the benefits) of a school community.	You can enroll your kids in school, reaping the social benefits (and complications) of a school community—as well as regular separation from your kids.
Due to limited time in each place, a deeper experience of community and culture will take a concerted effort, and may not feel organic.	An abundance of time allows you to take part in the natural rhythm of a local culture's ongoing and seasonal activities.

You can always look forward to the next new exciting place, and saying goodbye to each one likely won't be too painful a tug on your heartstrings.	You are stuck to a degree, leaving much of the planet left to discover. When your year is up, emotional attachment will likely make it difficult to leave.
Unless you limit your travels to countries of the languages you speak or are actively learning, extensive communication will require finding those who speak your language.	Unless you go to an English-speaking country, you must get comfortable using another language—and accept all the challenges (and rewards) that come with that.
After a while, many of the places you visit could become somewhat of a colorful blur.	You'll become deeply familiar with a place—possibly to the point of boredom (and ideally affection).
At the end of your travels you will have sampled a wide array of cultures and will feel a sense of accomplishment, having added a rich tapestry of memories to your life story.	At the end of your year you'll have a deep treasure trove of memories that will add texture to your life, but a host of world travels won't be part of it.

One choice is not better than the other. It's simply a matter of what you want your predominant experience to be. Circling the globe doesn't mean you won't make personal connections to the various cultures, just like staying in one place doesn't mean you won't travel. Whatever you choose, there will be times when the grass looks greener, when you might wish you had chosen the other option. Whether you push forward on a 'round-the-world plan or a one-special-place plan, your next steps involve some serious research.

HOMING IN ON WHERE TO GO

Researching where to go can be time-consuming unless you already know the precise location your year abroad dream beckons. Otherwise, follow some basic guidelines as you narrow in on your plan.

Multiple Locations

If your dream is to travel the globe, get out your world map. But before you plot your course—the ways and routes of which are myriad—consider the following:

- If you haven't already explored what others covered in their 'round-the-world adventures, seek out their stories. Read books written by folks who have conquered a portion of the planet, a couple of which are listed in the Appendix. Settle in at your computer and go down that rabbit hole of the Internet. Google "travel around the world + year" and you'll be overwhelmed with results.

- Instead of spending an entire day sifting through endless links, narrow down your returns by further defining your situation. Add key words to shape the returns you get (such as "family," "children," or "teens"). Are you a "history" buff? Is your family "active" or bent on an "educational" experience? If you're an artist, add the word "artist" or "art" into the mix. During this process, you'll discover countless blogs created by people who have done a version of what you hope to do. You'll also find websites of companies or organizations that offer something. Your job is to sift through the treasure trove of voices and find ones that resonate with you. The world—and the search terms—are your oyster.

- While you will forge your own unique path on this adventure, you don't need to reinvent the wheel when planning an itinerary. Learn from others. Consider what matters to you and dig deeper through the data on the Internet. If budget is of utmost importance, add "budget" to your search terms. You may find some off-the-beaten-path towns you weren't aware of. If you're trying to avoid extreme weather, take aim with the appropriate search terms. Chisel out potential routes and play with them.
- If your plan includes kids who are mature enough to have an opinion, involve them in the research process so they too are invested in the adventure.
- Use a tool like Evernote and create lists, folders, and a basic research plan you can build on over the coming months.

Single Location

If you're not sure whether to pursue a trip 'round the world or to settle in one special place, I encourage you to explore the latter. An extended stay in one location can become an experience of a lifetime. In our culture, *where* we live is usually decided for us—either by birth or by job opportunities. But to live someplace simply because you *want* to can create a new affection-filled chamber in your heart, which will weave itself into your personal history in a way continuous travel can't.

As you explore your possible where, it helps to go back to your Why. What do you seek by leaving your country for a year? Will certain characteristics of another place "feed" you, both individually and as a family? Practical considerations come into play as well, such as the following overarching components.

Visa

Some countries make it easy to obtain a work or residence visa. Others promote only short-term tourist visas. Certain countries may offer dual citizenship to those with a direct bloodline. Furthermore, some consulates have friendlier reputations than others when granting (or denying) visa applications. We'll cover visas in Chapter 5, but it's worth noting now as it can influence your geographical target.

Expense

Conventional wisdom holds that cities are more expensive than small towns. Likewise, countries or continents vary widely in cost. Norway, for example, is strikingly expensive, even compared to France or Italy. Asia and South or Central America, however, tend to be much more affordable than Europe in general. To get a sense for the cost of various places, use the search terms "cost of living" + index + [country] as you scan possibilities.

Factor in the price of everyday transportation too. Don't assume that buying or renting a car for twelve months will be a piece of cake, or even legal as a noncitizen. If you live in a dense city with good public transportation, you might be fine renting a car on an as-needed basis, which would offset the expense of a city. Yet living in a more affordable small town—*without* easy access to a car—might be too stifling for the year abroad of your dreams.

And then there's health care. Depending on the country and the type of visa you can get, you might hit the jackpot with access to low-cost, state-subsidized health care. Or your visa might mandate that you spend a significant amount for private health insurance.

Language

If you want regular contact with English speakers, go somewhere with strong tourism. Conversely, if you hope to learn the local language, head away from the tourists. For example, we often got confused looks when we told people we were living in Genoa, a city not popular for travel. But it was perfect for language learning because locals weren't primed to break out in English upon learning we were American.

Some countries excel at multilingualism, which usually includes English as it's the standard business language. If having a greater language barrier is more of a problem than an enjoyable quest for you, think carefully about your destination in this regard.

Familiarity of Culture

Only you can intuit how far out of the comfort zone your family will remain happy. As you consider your goals for the year, your cultural divining rod might pull you toward a more Westernized area. Something as simple as having easy access to your kids' favorite comfort foods from time to time could be crucial.

Or perhaps it's the opposite: You know in your heart of hearts that only an absolutely novel location is worth the effort if you're going to upend your life for a while.

Wherever it falls on the spectrum of familiar to exotic, explore the heck out of your potential locale online so you can try it on for size. While a year is fleeting, the place you target should still feel like a fit.

What If You Really, Really, Really Want to Go 'Round the World AND Stay in One Special Place?

Despite the laws of physics, you refuse to choose between continuous travel and staying put. Would you be happy with a compromise?

There are a million ways to experience the year abroad, including creating your own sampler plate version. Andrea and Dan Pether, along with their three kids, did just that. They divided up their sabbatical, starting first in their own backyard when they road-tripped across the western United States for three months.

Then they bought a van in New Zealand and participated in the WWOOFER (wwoof.net) program, where they worked on various organic farms in exchange for room, board, and being part of the community. After a few months traversing New Zealand, they headed for an adventure in Mexico, where they settled in to learn Spanish.

Another option to bridge both possibilities: Create a home base, then travel for weeks at a time. This is what the Maroney family did for a year. They jumped through hoops to obtain a French visa and first set up house in a town where they had friends. After settling in for a while, they took off for various parts of Europe, spending days, weeks, or months at a time in Ireland, Italy, England, Germany, Turkey, Greece, and more—but always circling back to France.

The possibilities are endless for where you go and how you design your extended time abroad. But if a compromise doesn't cut it for you, a little more introspection might help. Ask yourself:

- Do I get jazzed thinking about where to go next more than I feel depleted by the notion of repeated packing and unpacking?
- Does a new routine with new stimuli thrill me more than the ease of the familiar comforts me?
- Do I resonate more with "go deep and immerse as a specialist" or "be a jack of all trades, master of none"?

Don't count on having hard, set answers to these questions. You're aiming for the deeper self-reflection to let you know which direction your inner compass needle favors.

Regardless of this rigorous decision-making process, there may be other more personal factors that will determine where you spend your year abroad. Distant relatives? An offer for free or low-cost housing? A particular school for your kids?

Once you've gathered adequate information, simply sit still with your thoughts and feelings. Allow yourself to hear more distinctly the "someplace" that calls you. And if you aren't the meditative type, well… you can always ask the travel gods to guide your hand as you toss your darts onto a world map.

However you home in on the where—whether you envision a year of multiple locations, one special place, or a hybrid experience—at this stage you are digging into research. You are pinning or bookmarking locales and gathering information on places you'll circle back to as you do more hard-core planning. This can be a major project—especially as you start weaving in other aspects of planning your year abroad. So instead of binge watching the latest Netflix craze, adopt the mindset that your part-time gig in the coming months is to make this adventure happen.

Accepting Trade-Offs

In the previous chapter, while you were in the-sky's-the-limit mode, I urged you to put obstacles aside. But now, as you pull focus a bit more, compromise comes into the picture. While it would be nice to have it all and find the perfect location that meets all your needs, the truth is that every choice is a trade-off. You are limited not only by hard fact (North Korea is off the table given current geopolitics) but also by how much ease and comfort you're willing to sacrifice.

For example, you might relish frolicking near a warm, sunny beach in Central America for a year. But you have a fantastic opportunity to work in your field—albeit in Sweden, where for months the sun may only peek out on occasion. What trade-off are you ready to make?

Or, using these same two locations, maybe you're the world's number one ABBA fan, chomping at the bit to live in Scandinavia—but the cost of living there is no match for your bank account. But in Central America you could stretch out your savings for at least twelve months. Where are you prepared to compromise? How far will you go to find a means of earning money in the land of the "Dancing Queen"?

And sometimes you won't know you're making a trade-off until it happens, which is what happened for us. When we opted for Genoa, a medium-sized city with adequate public transit, we decided to forgo the hassles of a car. We knew that in an urban center plenty of cultural amenities would be a bus ride away. And our daughters would be able to continue with their kung fu and Irish dance activities, both available in the area.

But when we got settled and it came time to register for classes, it turned out the Irish dance studio met on the outskirts of the city. It meant over an hour-long bus ride *and* a twenty-minute walk to get there. The kung fu class had similar timing and bus route challenges. And by then other distractions kept us so busy it wasn't worth the effort. Instead, both girls did a tae kwon do class, which we mixed in with some group singing lessons and *ginnastica artistica*. All-new activities to go with an all-new life in a new country.

These are minor compromises, to be sure. But the bottom line is, whether you're deciding between an adventure 'round the world or in one special place—or whether you're deciding *which* special place to choose—every choice comes with trade-offs. To move your plan forward, you'll need to pick a direction and run with it. And you can take solace in knowing that whatever trade-offs you make, you won't feel their effects so much when you're living in the moment.

THE BIG WHEN: WHEN TO GO

Much of your decision on the *when* aspect of your year abroad will depend on your situation and circumstances. The big things— such as your financial resources, your career or job, your family commitments, even your health—will play a part in determining when you can extract yourself from your current life to journey overseas for a year.

The unknowns can loom over you like a dark cloud. You might be tempted to wait for the clouds to part and the angels to herald that magic moment called "the time is right." Resist this. There will always be something on the horizon—a job promotion, a big family event, a school year you can't miss—that will interfere with ideal timing. In order not to succumb to the myth of perfect timing, muster the courage to part those clouds and find your opening.

Only you can know your personal best timing for this adventure. But if kids are in the picture, some considerations will help you aim for your family's bull's-eye, depending on their ages. The classic question that comes up: Is it better to go when children are little or when they're older? The answer: It all depends. Putting aside the possibility of homeschooling (for now), let's explore different scenarios.

The Year Abroad with Young Children, Pre-School Age

You can avoid the hassle of looking for a school, or disrupting your kids' education once they've started school, if you do the year abroad before your children reach the age of five or six. This timing offers you great freedom to travel, not having to adhere to any school schedule. Ditto for finding housing: You won't be limited by the need to live close to a particular school.

What's the trade-off if you avoid the school years? Not being part of a school community makes it more challenging to connect with the local population, since you won't be part of a ready-made group. Nor will you have the built-in time away from your child during school hours. The lack of personal downtime will already be an issue with your family being more isolated, especially when you first arrive. Not having your child in school compounds the issue.

No school for your kids also reduces their chances of acquiring a second language, if that is your aim. On a similar note, if you want your kids to reap the benefits of soaking in another culture, going abroad when they're so young all but assures they won't have a significant memory of it.

Are there ways to combat these downsides? Sure. If you need more personal downtime, you can fold it in by finding a regular nanny or babysitter. Better yet, if you find a preschool or some type of day care, you might get some meaningful language and cultural immersion, or even an avenue into the local community. You'll still have the challenge of keeping the memory alive as your child gets older—but a preschool compromise could be ideal.

The Year Abroad with School-Aged and Older Kids

The older your kids are, the more they'll digest the year abroad. Within this wide age spread, every age has its pluses and minuses. Younger school-aged children will have an easier time meshing socially, while older ones will have a deeper sense of the magnitude of the experience. We often joked that we wanted to go when our daughters were old enough to have a memory of living in Italy but before they had raging hormones. We didn't want to deal with teenage boys on scooters chasing after them—or vice versa!

First or second grade tends to be easier for kids: They aren't as self-conscious; the local children are also new to the school experience; the language is simpler; the demands of school are gentler. This proved out with Mattea, our younger daughter, who went through second grade while we lived in Genoa. Our fifth-grader, Chiara, encountered more social challenges because the student friendships in her class were already formed and fixed by the tail end of elementary school.

Academic differences stood out too. Chiara needed more intensive language study for the first few months. Adjusting to more complicated subject matter in Italian proved frustrating.

But, curiously, despite these challenges, after we returned to the United States, Chiara held her experience in higher esteem than did Mattea. She better understood the value of our family adventure, and thus treasures it more to this day.

What about adolescent and teenaged kids? Depending on how attached your middle-schooler or older kids are to their peers, you might get pushback. Heck, even your younger kids may push back when they hear your plan to move to a foreign land for a year. After all, a year to a child is like a decade to adults.

If your teen is in the thick of high school, acceptable credits for transcripts and college applications might be of concern. Don't let that trip you up, though, particularly if your kid is up for the adventure or not wedded to the social scene at school. Several months of travel or life in a foreign country offers rich fodder for a standout college application essay. It's all in how you look at it.

I will delve into the school issue in Chapter 5, but if you are considering the year abroad with high school kids, I recommend Maya Frost's book, *The New Global Student: Skip the SAT, Save Thousands on Tuition, and Get a Truly International Education.* Frost makes a strong case for independent study abroad as she recounts her family's experience taking their four daughters out of the country during their teen years. I guarantee it will open your mind to how bringing your older kids overseas for an extended period could be the best decision you ever make.

The Other Kind of "When to Go"

No matter your kids' age, the other when factor is *what time of year*. Logic would dictate a summer arrival, with a return a year later, after completing a full school year. But if you end up south of the equator, like the Vaughn family who spent a year in Argentina, your child would be arriving in the middle of the school year and returning home in a higher grade than their peers. In that scenario you might strategically enroll your children in a lower grade upon arrival so they reenter the same grade as their peers. Or not. Maybe you adjust backward and figure they'll overlap in subject material.

Whatever your situation with timing, school, travel, and meshing with different cultural expectations, you will have no choice but to roll with the punches. Think of it as conditioning or building stamina for other challenges you'll encounter as you engineer the year abroad.

HOW LONG OF A WHEN?

I wrote this book with a year in mind as the target length. Whether it's the perfect length for such an adventure is debatable, but it's a clean unit of time that encompasses four seasons. It's long enough to feel substantial, but short enough to reenter a life that took years to build, one you presumably want to return to. Like everything else in this amorphous goal of doing a year abroad, however, it all depends on your situation. That includes your work, finances, kids, goals, dreams, and how you envision your year. And if an entire orbit around the sun doesn't work for you, it's worth exploring other measures of time.

Three Months

Eking out a three-month getaway might be all you can manage. If that's the case, then go for it and don't look back. You won't regret it. Three months is a typical length for a tourist stay, often with no visa required. Simply show up, hang out, and leave within ninety days. View it as a lengthy vacation. But be sure to confirm the rules and requirements of the countries you're considering before you plan.

Pros and cons? You'll give up integrating into the deeper community, going to school (aside from short-term language or miscellaneous classes), and learning the nuances of the culture. But you will get a taste for the year abroad and even start to form friendships if you make the effort. Such a fractional year away might prove to be a big fat tease, though one that could motivate you to return. Or it could inspire you to achieve something similar in another locale during a different year. A quarter-year abroad is nothing to sneeze at.

Four to Nine Months

When it comes to time abroad, I'm a fan of "more is better." If you go to the trouble of obtaining a visa, why not stay long as possible? If you're doing this to immerse in a second language, get as big of a stretch as you can. And if your kids will attend school, try to cover a period that will include trips, performances, or significant festivals—in order to maximize the cultural "wow." A solid goal would be to integrate with the community during whatever length your stay.

Ten Months to Two Years

A greater duration lets you settle in. Your return-home date is far enough out that it isn't staring you in the face. You can register your kids for a full school year, do some traveling, and spend holidays with locals as you develop friendships. When you put in such extended time, you become part of the fabric of the community. And it'll be hard to leave when you go. But it isn't *so* long that coming back means starting over in your hometown. Any longer than this and you may start to become less attached to your home town while further settling in to your new one. The longer you stay past a year, the more your year abroad will seem like a permanent move, which is a whole other can of worms.

ℓℓℓ

Much of this consideration doesn't apply if you plan to travel the world (or a part of it). With location hopping you aren't counting on building a relationship with a single society or the people in it. But wherever you are on the spectrum—from three months to over a year—the shorter the period, the more it will feel like an extended vacation. The longer you're out trekking the globe, the more it becomes a way of life. In any scenario the time will fly, leaving only memories. Your challenge is to figure out how best to make the richest memories—and consequently drive the most meaningful growth for you and your family.

eelee

SAVE IT FOR SOMEDAY TIPS

- Become a regular investigator of global destinations: read articles; talk to friends who travel; digest world news from the perspective of a potential resident; watch travel documentaries. In sum, better inform yourself so that when you're ready to plan, a particular location will be at the forefront.
- Talk with people who have done a year abroad. Listen to their stories; learn their process; take notes.
- Bring up the possibility with your kids that someday you could live in another part of the world for a short while. Share your enthusiasm as you plant the seed. Train *them* to be global investigators too!
- Don't be shy about bringing up your goal of living overseas someday. People might categorize it as a mere pipe dream, but when you put your plans in action, no one will be shocked. And you might even reap the benefit of gathering key contacts as the word leaks out.

CHAPTER THREE

MAKE A COMMITMENT TO FOLLOW THROUGH ON YOUR DREAM

ONCE YOU COMMIT TO doing something, it becomes a priority in your life. It becomes real. Things might still happen without a commitment. But when you actually make a pledge—to yourself, or outwardly—it means that, by gosh, come hell or high water, you will succeed in some way at whatever it is you're committing to.

As you build on this vision of living overseas, you might ask yourself, Am I just toying with this idea, or am I really going to do it? I know I did. How easy it was to daydream of taking walks on ancient medieval pathways, or ordering my caffè macchiato at a bar like a savvy local! Committing to the actual process of moving to Italy zapped the fun out of the fantasy in many ways.

It's easy to project and idealize without knowing everything involved. Think having babies, getting married, owning a home. Tedious work is often obscured by the stock image of a happy couple playing with a bouncy, smiling baby in the picture-perfect garden of a charming house that needs no repairs. The fantasy part never includes the poopy diapers or leaky roof.

Same goes for the dream of living abroad. It's much easier to fantasize about the villa in Provence surrounded by dancing fields of lavender than it is to endure the stress of procuring the château. And often the endgame looks far different from the pretty postcard version.

But if you've come this far in life, chances are you've matured to the point of knowing that (a) success doesn't come without hard work and persistence, and (b) things don't always turn out exactly as you plan. The acceptance of such basic truths as a fundamental reality, coupled with your resolve to do the year abroad, will propel you far in achieving your goal. Once you commit, things begin to shift and magic starts to happen.

THE FIRST LEAP

That initial leap of committing to your dream is by far the hardest step. And you will have to do it twice—first mentally, and then physically.

Think of doing the year abroad as climbing a mountain. Let's assume you don't have the benefit of a well-resourced HR department to set you up with a cushy expat deal. Your aim: to reach the mountain peak. The one essential provision is determination. All the other necessities we'll discuss in following chapters—but the constant aiming and pushing onward are crucial. This is not easy. Much less so if you're disinclined to ask for help.

Each step you conquer in reaching your goal of living overseas has you outside of your comfort zone. Your commitment manifests as going out on a limb and getting okay with being uncomfortable in the unknown. And then venturing out on a *different* limb to become okay with *another* unknown. You commit and repeat, pushing the boundaries of your comfort zone again and again. And once you go public with your pledge, two opposing things occur:

1. The obstacles on the terrain ahead come into focus, so you see clearly what needs to be moved aside or worked around. Heck, people will take special pains to point out obstacles in your plan to leave the country for a year. They'll tell you it's too hard, that your children and/or your career will suffer. In varying degrees of volume "Don't do it" hums in the background and reverberates from every direction. But you can learn to use this naysaying to your advantage.

2. People who sense your seriousness in doing the year abroad will cheer you on. When you put it out there, aid arrives, often at just the right time. Helpful indicators appear around you, and you get quite good at reading their signs.

BEYOND A VERBAL COMMITMENT

The act of committing must take place with your mind, body, and soul—not only with words. Recent studies[4] show that sometimes announcing one's objective can reduce the chances of achieving it. While stating your intentions *might* hold you accountable and draw others into helping you, it also can have the opposite effect, and prevent you from realizing your goal.

In experiments where one's ego stood to gain from announcing one's intention, the reward felt from making the announcement alone diminished the motivation to complete the goal. For example, if you declare that you're going to diet to lose twenty pounds, you're likely to get immediate encouragement: "Good for you!" "That's a healthy target; you'll rock it!" Studies show that this often leaves the person feeling as though they've already achieved the goal at some level, and so their desire to work toward their true objective dwindles.

In the case of the year abroad, once you declare your intention, you might become "the family who is going to sail around the world" or "the year in Chile people" or what have you. And this could inadvertently hinder your efforts. Your subconscious might enjoy a false sense of satisfaction, as though you've already achieved the status of having done a year abroad.

While these studies suggest that sometimes it's better to keep your goals to yourself and not tell anyone your intentions, that's not an option with the year abroad. Others will need to know your plans as you realize various stages of your vision. And the deep, personal Why you defined earlier has the power to inoculate you from the subconscious setbacks described in these studies. Coming back to your Why should continue to fuel your motivation and keep you pushing forward, overriding any such psychosocial effects.

LET THE MAGIC HAPPEN

The fun part about committing to the year abroad—and I mean committing deep in your heart, not only with your words—is that magic happens. And if "magic happens" is too woo-woo for you, swap it out for "things start falling into place."

In our own story, I was a couple months out from a reconnaissance trip, still unsure where in Italy we wanted to go. Instead of throwing a dart at a map of the Boot, we decided we would limit our choices to places with the most fitting school possibilities. Because our girls were several years into the Montessori method, we figured seeking out a Montessori elementary school in Italy would allow a smoother transition there and back. A surprising dearth of choices meant I had to narrow our options to a small handful of locales, adding Genoa to my itinerary at the last minute.

It was early January, and I was standing at a birthday party making small talk with a group of women I didn't know terribly well. When the conversation shifted to my upcoming scouting trip, I mentioned I'd be heading to Genoa. It turned out one of the women lived there part-time for her work. When I told her I was going to visit the Scuola Mazzini elementary school, her eyes popped open. "That's right down the street—literally—from my apartment," she said in her thick Italian accent. Then I let her know my travel dates for Genoa, and we discovered we'd overlap for a few days. She offered to take me to the school, which ultimately facilitated our enrolling there.

Months later, once we targeted Genoa as our location abroad, similar coincidences would occur. Someone knew someone, and those connections begat other connections. This infused that arduous mountain trek with wonder and ease.

Bridget Kresse echoes the sentiment to "follow the magic" and not rely on mere planning and logistics. She reflects, "It's kind of like that scene in *Star Wars* where they say, 'Use the force, Luke.' You'll feel like you are open to all the possibilities in the universe." You might even think of it as an enchanted force field you can tune in to for your benefit.

Now, I'm not saying you should sit back and wait for a wizard in the sky to perform her miracles. In our case, we worked hard to put our dream out there and do what was necessary. For example, the party where I met Alessandra Gardino, the woman from Genoa, was at the home of another Italian friend. Since my attraction to Italy was ages old, it meant I found myself in situations connected to the local Italian community from time to time. So I was already swimming in friendly waters, which facilitated the synchronicity that worked in our favor.

Your intention can set you up for success in a similar way if you let it. And when others sense your determination, they'll whip out their little wands, consciously or otherwise.

What transpires for you and what *will* transpire for you is only limited by your imagination—and by how far you're willing to exceed the bounds of your comfort zone.

selee

SAVE IT FOR SOMEDAY TIPS

- Nurture the ability to make stuff happen in your life. Commit to accomplishing something, however small, just to prove to yourself you've got the mojo. Even simple things, like learning to cook a new dish or organizing your closet, build your "I will follow through" muscle.
- Think about your lofty someday goal of living abroad and break that mountain into tiny mounds. Vow to do something minor that feeds into the dream. For example, pledge to take a language class. Or invite people over who have gone to foreign locales that interest you. And then see those smaller climbs through to completion.
- Consider mentioning to your superiors at work that you plan on taking a sabbatical in X number of years down the road. They may assume it's a pipe dream, but as the date approaches no one can claim surprise. A verbal commitment, however loose, might free you up to do early legwork for your year abroad.
- If you manage your own business, committing now might mean you consider how you'll replace yourself during your sabbatical. Then, as you hire people or take on new clients, do it factoring in your future temporary absence.

CHAPTER FOUR

FIND AND KEEP GOOD COMPANY

UNTIL NOW YOU'VE BEEN researching various aspects of your planned adventure, no doubt related to your target country or travel path. But once you commit to making your dream happen, the next logical step is to get the word out. And I don't just mean blurting out your plans in a spontaneous social media post. Rather, be thoughtful about your announcement. Letting your intentions be known in earnest and with focus serves a dual purpose:

1. It reveals who your supporters are—and who your naysayers are.
2. It allows you to build a community of ambassadors, who will facilitate your transition abroad.

I call these supporters, naysayers, and ambassadors *the company you keep.* Their attitude, knowledge, and support (or lack thereof) affect you, whether or not you agree with their messages. And while we can't *always* cherry-pick the company we keep, we *can* quiet the negative voices while amplifying the helpful ones.

DROWN OUT THE NAYSAYERS

I don't know any family who's done the year abroad without battling naysayers to some degree. Naysayers might appear as loved ones who worry for your well-being or as co-workers who are envious. They can be anyone in your sphere who feels threatened, even subconsciously, by your determination and self-empowerment to follow a dream. You will sense their unsupportive energy, even if they give you conflicting messages.

As you put the word out about your plan, some people will voice concern or even dire warnings regarding your year abroad. You'll hear that your kids will fall behind in their schooling, that your retirement fund will take a dramatic hit if you pause your income earning, or even that it's irresponsible to take your family out into the "dangerous" world.

I remember mingling at a party several months before we left for Italy, when a man I didn't even know had an extreme reaction to my mention of our plans. "You can't do that! You can't just suspend your life and move to Italy for a year!" he harped. At that point I laughed it off, but had my husband and I been in a more vulnerable stage of our planning, it might not have been so funny.

These negative messages are almost always projections of other people's insecurities regarding their own life choices. One person I spoke with, who did a ten-month adventure abroad with his family, told a story of catching snark from family friends: "Must be nice to just pick up and travel for the year." Ironically, these same folks drove a luxury car, belonged to a country club, and owned a vacation home.

It bears stating that everyone chooses and prioritizes where they put their money. It's easy to assume something is wrong with your choice when it's outside the mainstream. But why is saving for a year abroad perceived as a forbidden luxury when joining a country club or owning a second home is deemed acceptable, despite costing the same, if not more? Buying an experience is no less valid than buying a thing.

Your aim is to be unapologetic about following your dream—while using any criticism to bolster your resolve or perfect your plan.

Tracey Carisch, author of *Excess Baggage: One Family's Around-the-World Search for Balance*, also endured negative reactions when she announced her family's goal to take an extended international journey. To her, talking about the trip gave it more focus and encouraged her to confront the good, the bad, and the ugly. She reflects, "Even the pessimistic comments are helpful, because they're simply things you had rolling around in your own head to some extent. By hearing them and responding to them, you work through your own doubts and reaffirm how important this trip is to your family."[5]

Michelle Damiani, former American expat, clinical psychologist, and author of *Il Bel Centro: A Year in the Beautiful Center,* advises, "Don't listen to naysayers. People may not understand, but it's not your job to make them understand. It's your job to follow the path of your intention."

At some level, dealing with the chorus of naysayers is akin to living through the awkward adolescent years when *not* wearing the popular clothing brand put you in the camp of "other." Donning the handmade dress your grandmother lovingly stitched made you an oddball. But the truth is, wearing *anything* with confidence makes you the cool kid. And if you can shift to knowing you already *are* the cool kid, you'll pass the naysayer test with flying colors.

If you're super sensitive to the naysayer voices that surround you, remember that you live your life based on your priorities, not someone else's. Your best defense is to nip them in the bud with a kind but firm response. And while you don't owe anyone an explanation for your plans, if you choose to engage, these three types of responses can be effective at disarming the negativity:

1. Offer thanks for the concern. If you want to—though you are not obligated—throw them a bone to allay their concerns:

   "Yes, we know we may have to push out retirement an extra year. We are thinking of it as a year of retirement now instead of later."

   "We plan to be in touch with junior's teacher here to make sure he's on track when we return."

2. Arm yourself with knowledge and general truths. If you are so inclined, offer to send back-up data:

   "From everything I'm reading, people who take sabbaticals report a boost in creativity and energy, and even a renewed commitment to their work.[6] And more companies are seeing the benefit of offering a sabbatical." (Odds are high what follows is: "I wish my company offered a sabbatical.")

   "If you want to talk about safety, *leaving* the country might be the most rational choice. Did you know the US is ranked in the bottom third of peaceful countries? I can send you an article with statistics if you like."[7]

3. Counter with your opinion, which even if not mainstream, is still valid. No one can really argue with an opinion:

   "Actually, we believe learning a second language will offset any math our kids might fall behind on."

   "Our view is that traveling the world will pack a powerful punch in broadening our horizons for the next chapter of our lives. And it'll better inform the next steps in our careers."

With a little practice, responding swiftly to naysayers becomes as simple as swatting flies. This will allow you to preserve your energy for the more important work of finding and keeping *good* company. Because now it's time to build up your community of supporters and find your ambassadors.

FIND YOUR AMBASSADORS

A fundamental key to realizing your dream is to find ambassadors for the unique year abroad experience you're creating. And I don't mean in a literal title-holding sense. But anybody willing to connect with you can offer the benefit of their knowledge and experience. Like this book, they're eager to offer advice.

Based on what you learn from your ambassadors, you might tweak your itinerary before you go, or while you're traveling. Or you will gain insider tips regarding your target location. Such a network of contacts can also act as a safety net should you encounter any complications during your adventure.

Sure, the Internet offers an overabundance of useful (and often questionable) information to come to your aid for any of this. But nothing beats a contact through personal connections, or one found via the Internet, of course.

Who should you seek out as ambassadors?

- People who live in your target location. Once you know where you want to land, scout out folks (natives *and* expats) who live and work there as they are potential key ambassadors. For those planning a 'round-the-world year, pursue both those traveling a similar route you're considering as well as those living in places you hope to visit.
- People in your profession, if finding work in your field is a priority. Those who have already found a way to work abroad can shed light on where you might look, and perhaps even offer introductions.

- Mentors of all kinds. Search for anybody who's done a similar version of what you hope to do. Maybe they've lived where you're aiming to go, journeyed along an appealing travel route, or even have a similar situation as yours (such as kids the same age). They can offer you wisdom.
- Miscellaneous helpers and guides. At various points of your year abroad planning, you'll need recommendations and insights. For example, when it comes time to rent your house, you'll need an agent or manager. Or if you're looking at a language school, how will you determine the best one? Various single-issue contacts can prove just as helpful as big-picture ambassadors. One type often leads to the other.

The following steps comprise an open-ended process to discover and connect with potential ambassadors. Keep in mind that making ambassador contacts may not happen in a logical order. It's likely to be a messy, random process—sometimes frustrating, and other times ridiculously easy.

Carve Out Focused Time

The adage "it's a full-time job to find a job" also rings true for making the year abroad happen. It may not be forty-hour-a-week work, but you'll need to carve out varying amounts of time at different stages of the process. Think of it as hunting down your dream job, following similar steps:

- Research
- Ask questions, both general and pointed
- Network
- Communicate clearly
- Be persistent
- Thank those who make the effort to engage with you

(and toughen up when people say no or are otherwise flakey, as you will encounter plenty of both)

Create a Focused Introduction Message

Whether you have a specific group in mind you'd like to connect with or you cast the net wide, you'll need to create an introduction and an ask. Your message should be well-crafted, succinct, warm, and include:

- Some description of who you are, including family members who will join you
- Your target location, however specific you can be
- Target dates
- What you're looking for (Housing? Work? School? Community contacts? Volunteer opportunities?)
- Your contact info
- Gratitude/appreciation for a response or a referral
- A translated version below the original message if your destination has a dominant language other than English

In our case, since we weren't wed to a specific location in Italy, we first aimed to find the right school for our kids. Our initial inquiry blast asked if anyone knew anyone who might have Montessori school connections in Italy. And though that message did not match us up with a school or a city, it turned up contacts that led to further connections. It also helped us get our game on when it came to talking about our year abroad plan—all of which helped build our community of ambassadors.

Our initial outreach had a specific request, but it also welcomed general responses. You should tailor your introduction message in a similar fashion. A generic "We would like to live in another country. Anybody have connections anywhere?" kind of blast might yield a handful of replies, but a more specific, personalized inquiry is more likely to spark quality communication. A focused message also communicates you're serious about the year abroad plan and not just fantasizing. You want people to know they won't be wasting their time if they make the effort to help you.

Once you've honed a message in your authentic voice, get set to reach out to your social contacts within however wide a circle you're comfortable. Prepare an email and/or social media blast that can be forwarded by others. With any luck, this will connect you to a few friends of friends able to offer help, advice, or further contacts.

Contact Your Affiliate Groups

Your next strategy is to knock on the doors of any group you already belong to, adjusting your introductory message according to the person or group you're contacting. These might include:

- **Alumni associations**. Many institutions of higher learning (high schools too) have an alumni directory categorized by location. You want to hang out in Spain? Search your alumni directory for graduates who live in Spain. Even if you are targeting a particular city, contact alums in other cities as you never know who they know.
- **Professional associations**. Take advantage of any organized group related to your work. (This assumes by now you are public in your professional circles regarding your plan to live overseas.)
- **Local organizations connected to your destination area**. If you aim to be in Thailand, for example, and there's a local Thai culture club, reach out. If your plan is to sail around the world, introduce yourself to the nearest boating club. Maybe someone there will have a friend who's sailed around the world and is willing to advise you.

- **Foreign-language speakers of your destination country**. Assuming you're already dabbling in the (non-English) language of the country you're targeting, reach out to any clubs or groups focused on that language. And if you aren't yet dabbling in that language, sign up for a class!
- **Church or volunteer groups**. Any such organization you're comfortably associated with is worth shouting out to. And a shared belief or cause can create a powerful synergy propelling you forward.

In all the cases mentioned above—and any others you come up with—you are already part of the community in some fashion. This is your solid "in" that should garner a strong reply.

Whether you send a tailored email, post on a board, or circulate a short introduction linked to a website you've created, your goal is to get the word out in a shareable way. So check privacy settings on any posts if you want them to go beyond your circles. Often the person who helps you with housing, schools, finding a job, or getting a visa will be a degree or two removed from the person who reads your initial inquiry.

Once you've sounded the trumpets that you're embarking on the epic adventure of living abroad, the chatter among your friends and family will commence. Hurray if your inbox is flooded with an immediate onslaught of responses! But don't despair if only a few responses trickle in at first. Even if you've cast the net wide, it only takes one crucial contact to help advance your quest.

No matter how many replies you receive, respond to each one with at least a thank you. When you follow up with those individual referrals, explain how you're connected to them (for example, "Your sister is a close colleague of my cousin Mary"). Whether you share a friend in common, had the same major in college, or happen to have visited their hometown once, mention it. If you're able to create a deeper personal connection, do it.

This may seem like Networking 101, but it bears emphasizing. Personal relationships are the stuff that life is made of, and are what will foster your goal of expat life.

Target Social Media Groups, Forums, and Bloggers

Besides reaching out to your *personal* affiliate circles, your aim is to engage with dedicated groups in *any* platform or online forum you're comfortable using. And if you aren't engaged in social media and still only have an anemic number of helpful contacts, then you need to get with the program.

Although Facebook has been the most popular platform in the last dozen years, a quick search for "social networking websites" will yield others. Related types of sites include:

- General expat forums/websites[8]
- Expat sites catering specifically to those in your intended region
- Blogs that resonate with your year abroad plan
- Interest groups or clubs related to your destination or plan

Sharpen your focus to determine your best identifiers, such as "world travelers," "sabbatical seekers," "Americans in Poland," or "raising kids abroad." The possibilities are endless, and you'd be surprised at what already exists—on LinkedIn, as Facebook groups, blogs, forums within broad or country-specific expat sites, and more.

Be creative and exhaustive with your search terms in order to find the best-fitting groups, pages, or blogs. The better the fit, the more likely it will have participants able to guide *you*. Whether you "meet" someone in a comment feed or an actual blogger via a contact form, you never know who you will connect with. Your goal is to wend your way into any online community or conversation that allows you to chat and interact with other participants.

When I was trying to uncover useful data on the Montessori schools I'd found, I commented on a two-year-old blog post. I subscribed to an Italian parent newsletter I stumbled upon. I even joined a Facebook group for teachers who aspired to train in Italy for their Montessori certification. Each effort offered a glimmer of insight: a vote of confidence for one school, or a lackluster review of another. Because I had *zero* knowledge of the school system in Italy, every tidbit was valuable and gave me something to inform my next step.

Certain communities might require that you request to join— and for these you'll post a brief introduction, explaining why you'd like to participate in their group. Other sites may charge a modest fee to help maintain costs. A quick search might yield reviews for such a pay site, telling you whether it's worth the fee.

Build Your Network of Relationships

When you're part of an online forum, it's like lurking on the edges of a party until you join a worthwhile discussion. You have to figure out your jumping-in point—or your conversation-starter question. Once the ice is broken, these virtual settings are great for fostering a helpful network of allies.

But like any relationship you build, it requires effort. Show you're listening by responding to others' posts. Offer tips, links, or other contacts when appropriate. If you tap into the relevant groups and become active, online and social media acquaintances could be your magic elixir of contacts that bridges you to your future community, which is what happened for Jeremy and Christine Vyska.

Jeremy and Christine wanted to make a conscious choice about where they would live and raise their child, regardless of country. And so they began a long and involved research period. They started with the OECD's Better Life quiz (oecdbetterlifeindex.org), which pointed them toward Scandinavia as being a good fit. After looking more closely at criteria that mattered to them—climate, economy, population density—they zeroed in on Gothenburg, Sweden.

But before they could commit to pulling up their American stakes and moving overseas, they delved deeper, wanting to understand the roots of the culture they were considering calling home. To do this, however, they had to talk to Swedes. The only problem was, they didn't know any.

Enter the Internet. Finding blogs and websites that allow commentary and interactivity meant that, slowly but surely, connections could be made. Once Jeremy and Christine put the word out that they wanted to learn about the underpinnings of Swedish culture, folks they met online were only happy to oblige, even summoning their Swedish friends to the cause.

Conversations took place via Skype calls and even comment threads. At one point, Christine noticed a commenter from Sweden in a blog she followed and engaged him in a thread, hoping to gain insight about Sweden. And Jeremy, an avid gamer, struck up friendships with guildmates in the virtual *World of Warcraft*, which led to other introductions instrumental to their move.

Through these connections, Jeremy and Christine received help with an employment contract, in finding a coveted apartment, and even getting discounted shipping costs when they ultimately made the move to Sweden. The friendships they made during their research period are no longer virtual. And the commenter Christine originally engaged in a blog is now both a friend and neighbor.

Determination was the fundamental driving force that got the Vyska family to Scandinavia. Still, Jeremy reflects, "The friends we made online in advance of our move are probably what gave us the courage to actually make the leap." What started out in 2011 as a dream of moving to Sweden ended up as a reality in 2014. And those random Internet contacts helped create a smooth transition all around.

Although Jeremy and Christine sought to make a more permanent move, which is reflected in their lengthy and careful decision-making process, their story still applies to your adventure. The bridge-building they did to get overseas—and what I and many others did—follows similar steps as ones you'll take to realize your year abroad.

Some may bristle at the thought of collecting friends like baseball cards. Truth is, often your attempted engagement online will go nowhere. Other times, you might have a single exchange with someone who offers you a crucial—or useless—bit of information. But there's nothing artificial about online relationship building. It pretty much mirrors real life in that some communications might be superficial and sporadic while others might evolve into trusted friendships.

As you mine the Internet for potential ambassadors, maintain the mindset that the connections you make are fluid, like all human relationships. It also can't hurt to have a hopeful attitude, albeit one with limited expectations.

Don't Forget the "Real World"

Your offline contacts are no different from any virtual connections you make, except that they might hold more oomph. This is especially true when they are referred by close friends or colleagues. And meeting in person allows subtle cues to contribute to a richer interaction, which is always a good thing. You can increase the chances of building real-world allies by joining Meetups (meetup.com) in your hometown, taking a language class, attending cultural festivals celebrating your target country, and so on.

Remind yourself of the goal: to build relationships with those who can help you realize your dream of doing the year abroad.

Whether these relationships begin online or off matter less than what they bring to your quest. Anyone who knows more than you do about any aspect of living in your goal country, obtaining a visa, or traveling in particular parts of the world is a potential ally. This might sound cold and calculating, but it's not in the least. It's basic networking, just like that job hunt.

Consider a Reconnaissance Trip

One sure way to add those precious real-world ambassadors to your network is to take a reconnaissance trip. For those who have a single location in mind for the year abroad, it's possible to jump-start your planning with a short visit. Minimal research will give you the lay of the land and let you map out a trip. Going in person allows you to see potential flats, step foot into the schools, and meet people face to face.

I took a trip fifteen months in advance of our big move for the sole purpose of narrowing down a location within Italy by scouting the Montessori schools I discovered online. Ale, the woman I had lucked into meeting at the aforementioned party, whom I now call my dear friend, graciously escorted me into an elementary school I was eyeing.

I was so glad to have a local accompany me because my nerves were in high gear, dashing any hopes my Italian would sound remotely fluid. Ale navigated the school with ease, charming her way past the secretaries and into a couple of classrooms. The thirty-minute visit allowed me to get a feeling for the learning environment and chat with a few teachers.

One particularly warm and smiling teacher, Gabriella, invited me into her third-grade class and incorporated me into a geography lesson. She asked me where I was from, then with a decisive swoop lifted a slight boy up, directing him to point to the US West Coast on a roll-down classroom map.

With Ale's help, I stumbled my way through that visit, and I got the names of the teachers we met so I could follow up with thank-you notes. I did the same for the principal, who held the power to approve or deny our request to enroll. The rest of that scouting trip allowed me to compare not only schools but the vibe of potential towns as well. From those visits I gathered that

Perugia would be too small and remote for us, and that Como lacked the Italian "feel" we sought. Genoa—which had been a late addition to the list—felt just right. So we moved forward with more certitude.

Once we settled on Genoa, Ale offered to rent us her apartment for six months, and we pushed ahead with Scuola Mazzini. It turned out Gabriella was to be our eldest daughter's teacher, which enabled correspondence between Chiara and her future classmates in the months leading up to our arrival. The reconnaissance trip brought clarity to our plan and allowed for a smoother transition by finding key ambassadors for our year abroad.

Such an exploratory trip doesn't have to happen so far in advance to be effective. Erica and Rob Vaughn did reconnaissance to Argentina three months before their departure in order to decide on a town for their year abroad. After connecting with people—on Facebook, on blogs, through friends—they decided to spend a week each in Mendoza and Córdoba before deciding which city would become their temporary home.

Mendoza's location and beauty were seductive, but they had been warned that the community was insular and not super welcoming. Even folks in Mendoza espoused the virtues of Córdoba, effusively proclaiming how warm and inviting the people were. So by the time the Vaughns arrived at their second destination, they were already sold. The visit clinched it for Córdoba. They looked at houses and schools, and lined things up enough to make the move three months later without timidity.

Tips for a Successful Reconnaissance Trip
If you can swing a scouting trip (accrue those frequent flier miles!), keep these three things in mind:

1. Try to book appointments in advance. If you hope to get a lot out of a short visit, you'll need to be organized. Though not all cultures are big fans of

promptness and scheduling, they usually adjust for foreign visitors. If school scouting is part of your plan, at a minimum check scholastic calendars ahead of time to make sure they'll be in session. Try to confirm any visits before you arrive. And while you can't count on being able to pop in to places on a whim, don't be afraid to try.

2. Hire a translator or guide if needed. If you are going to a non-English-speaking country and are not comfortably fluent in the language, budgeting in a local guide or translator is money well spent. Your contacts on expat forums, or even apartment owners on Airbnb, should be able to find someone for you. At a minimum, consider bringing a translator with you to housing and school visits. While you may or may not comprehend what's being said, you'll want to ask and understand the subtle details—and a local bilingual will be able to convey crucial information that will go a long way in reducing your stress. A potential bonus is that your interpreter will become another source for future ambassador introductions, making it more than worth the cost.

3. Collect contact info for the people you meet. A gracious thank you sent afterward will remind them who you are and increase the chances they'll go out of their way to help you. This obvious gesture is doubly important if your reconnaissance location becomes your target spot for the year.

Pay It Forward

Part of finding and keeping good company is *being* good company. Think karma—and you don't have to target time in India to experience it. I may be going out on a limb for the purely practical reader—but the whole Golden Rule thing exists for a reason.

I'm not suggesting we should be helpful to others only because we'll get some benefit from them in return. But simply put: When you exude positive energy, it draws in others and everyone benefits. Though you don't always get to see the fruits of your generosity, sometimes it boomerangs right back to you, like it did for us in these two examples.

One of the final stumbling blocks of setting up our year abroad was getting our house rented. The rental income would be a crucial piece of the puzzle, making it possible for us to cover rent in Italy without dipping too much into our savings. And finding someone who wanted to rent a furnished house would be ideal, since we didn't want to clear out all our belongings and pay for storage.

Several months prior to our hunt for renters, I had received an inquiry on my website, which helped parents in Portland navigate their school options. A woman named Helen, in the Czech Republic of all places, asked me about schools because they were moving to Portland for a year while her husband, Hynek, would explore business opportunities. I took the time to offer my opinion and, while I was at it, asked if they had already secured housing.

One thing led to another, and during one of Hynek's business trips, he met us, checked out our house, and a furnished rental contract fell into place. I don't know that the stars could have aligned better for either of our families. Having them show us around Prague before we landed in Italy was frosting on the cake.

On that same Portland schools website, a woman named Elizabeth Petrosian left a comment on a post, casually mentioning she and her family were relocating to Portland *from* Italy. Well, I certainly couldn't let *that* go ignored. I offered to make local introductions for her—exactly what I would have relished if I were in her position. And several emails later, Elizabeth and I struck up a friendship.

Over the months of our planning and corresponding with teachers in Genoa, she would correct my Italian and give me the inside scoop on Italy's public school system. I ended up connecting Elizabeth to several friends who helped her family get established in Portland while we were in Genoa. Years later, we still see each other regularly and our kids enjoy a sweet friendship. (If you ever visit Portland, check out their delicious Tuscan restaurant, Burrasca.)

Skeptics among you may chalk these karmic examples up to sheer coincidence. And when you are trying to live your life *while also* planning for a big adventure, putting forth energy to pay it forward may seem like the least good use of your time. But generosity begets generosity. I dare you to test the theory.

SUSTAINING YOUR CIRCLE OF AMBASSADORS

As your mountain of tasks builds while you plan your year abroad, you will trip over plenty of challenges and problems that need solving (see Chapter 5). But the company you keep can make the process easier. Not only that, but you're creating a welcoming circle, however big or small, in advance of your arrival.

If you skew extrovert and easily dive into exchanges with people you don't know, then none of this ambassador-seeking will intimidate you. But if all this reaching out to "strangers who are friends we haven't met yet" brings on an allergic reaction, take heart. You always have a tool in your back pocket, ready to whip out. It will aid anyone who needs a boost to keep going. That is, returning to your Why.

Somewhere in your Why lurks a desire for personal growth; otherwise, you wouldn't be considering a year abroad. Nurture that growth by pushing the boundaries of your social comfort zone—because it's something you will do every single day during your yearlong immersion in a foreign land. And finding and keeping your circle of ambassadors can make a huge difference in how your year plays out.

At first it may feel like you're issuing excessive requests to your budding network of helpers and insiders. At worst, you'll be considered overeager and exuberant. But it's far more likely you'll be finding answers and solutions just when you need them. In no time you'll determine who your best go-to sources are for various aspects of your planning. And by being clear about what you're asking—and grateful in return—you'll become more efficient in gathering the appropriate information.

In the long run, while your plans progress, and even during your year away, expect to keep in regular contact with one or two ambassadors while following a few groups or forums online. Sustaining these connections should yield regular messages that prop you up and push you forward with your plans.

eelee

SAVE IT FOR SOMEDAY TIPS

- The most powerful thing you can do to prepare for your someday dream is learn to dial down the negative, draining messages in your life while increasing those that encourage and inspire. Yes, it's the company you keep—the friends and family you listen to—but it's also everything else you let into your head.

  Pay close attention to your media diet. If certain TV shows, radio shows, even musicians or authors leave you feeling drained, depressed, or anxious, change the channel and seek replacements that leave you hopeful and inspired.

  This goes for social media too. If you follow drama seekers who spew out negative energy that's difficult to tune out, hide or unfollow them. The negative voices drag you down more than you realize.

- If you skew introverted, start to push yourself in ways that let you exercise your extrovert muscle. Get comfortable communicating online. Leave comments and engage in conversations. Seek out like-minded people in any area of your life that feeds you.
- Scout ambassadors now even if it's in a passive way. People who have done a similar adventure, or who live or have lived where your someday dream calls you, can serve as a beacon, guiding you toward your eventual destination.
- Maintain connections to any affiliate groups you belong to and consider joining others that fit. These include clubs, professional networks, alumni associations, community organizations, and more. Pay those membership dues! Because when you're ready for someday, these groups can help build your network, which in turn will help you transition abroad.
- Start saving frequent flier miles and points for an eventual reconnaissance trip. That way, when it comes time to meet your good company, you'll be ready to fly there without the burden of a ticket purchase. By using credit cards and accumulated miles, you might even be able to cover the travel costs for the entire year abroad for you and your family. Explore sites such as extrapackofpeanuts.com, onemileatatime.com, or frugaltravelguy.com to learn the ropes of travel hacking.

Part Two: The Nuts and Bolts of Making Your Dream Happen

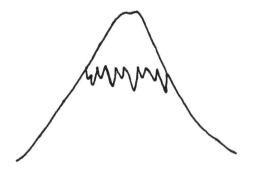

CHAPTER FIVE

CLIMB YOUR MOUNTAIN OF PRACTICAL DETAILS

HERE YOU ARE, STANDING at the base of an amorphous mountain. You know that when you reach the summit, exhilarating vistas and tantalizing explorations await. But the trek to the top is arduous and daunting, even though you have ambassadors to ease your passage.

The technical and practical tasks that comprise your journey to the year abroad will generally take about a year to complete. This includes much of the research mentioned thus far. Some hardy folks manage it in a few months, while others require more time. You see, the trail is one that only you can forge, and what you'll encounter is impossible to predict.

In this meaty book-within-a-book chapter, we'll go through

the biggest potential challenges so you can begin to get a handle on them. These areas include:

- Finances, including work and money
- Housing, abroad and home
- Schools, for your kids and/or language learning if applicable
- Visas
- Health and wellness, including pets
- Transportation while abroad
- Staying organized
- Making the final leap

Bit by bit, you'll tackle the hurdles, checking things off the list. Pretty soon you'll find you're a quarter of the way up the proverbial mountain. More stuff will get checked off, and you'll be halfway up. Be forewarned: When you look up to see how far you've yet to go—or you glance down to note how dizzyingly far you've come—you may face some existential freak-out moments.

You might discover something's not working as planned. Maybe the apartment you thought you had procured falls through, or some section of your visa application has a gaping hole. During those points on your trek, you might need to climb partway down the mountain in order to find a different path up, or perhaps you'll have to bushwhack your way through a thicket. But with commitment and determination, you'll get there.

I remember any number of freak-outs during the year we prepared for our adventure in Italy: a slippery communication with the owner of a potential flat, a noncommittal response about the girls enrolling at their school, the long stretch of no bites when renting our house. And the to-do list! It would suck the oxygen right out of me as thoughts swirled in my brain like a Category 4 hurricane: "*OMG! How will I ever get all this to fall into place?*

Is it really worth all this stress? Maybe we should just take a vacation instead. Aaaack!!"

If you experience some version of berserk (and you will), the only response is:

Deep Breath.

Break it down into small chunks.

Move forward.

One step

at

a

time.

FINANCES

Financing the adventure abroad tends to be the behemoth obstacle in most people's minds when they consider it in earnest. Almost everybody asks, "How much will this cost?"

It's impossible to answer that question with any kind of ballpark figure due to myriad permutations of factors: How many are you? How costly is your regular lifestyle? How simply are you willing to live? How expensive is your target location? Will you have access to public transportation? Will you have any income from renting out your house? Will you continue to work? How much travel will you do? And on and on…

What I can tell you about our own experience is that when we were living in Genoa we spent about 30 percent less than we normally do. And this was during a not-so-great period for the dollar (1 Euro was about $1.40 in US dollars. A year later, it was about $1.10!). Our purchasing habits were quite different, however.

We did not spend money as though we were in vacation mode (dining out, hotels, souvenirs, etc.) unless we were traveling outside Genoa. And over the course of our time in Italy, we bought a lot less stuff than we were in the habit of buying back home. This also meant we didn't have to pay to ship new items back.

(One gift of our year abroad was breaking out of that mindless consumerism American culture does so well.)

Another point of our reduced spending was with air travel. We managed to book the major flights to and from Europe for all four of us using frequent-flier miles. That alone saved us several thousand dollars. And for our travel within Europe, we flew cheap European airlines, which tend to cost a fraction of the major ones.

So as you project out financially, think about what kind of lifestyle you *need* to maintain versus what you're willing to live without. And then factor in how much income—if any—you'll bring in while you're away. The job conundrum can be a big hurdle for those who manage the year abroad. But with focus and intention, it is surmountable.

To Work or Not to Work?

A true sabbatical may exist for those in academia or those who have generous bosses and bank accounts. With proper planning, it may exist for you too. But for most people, *not* working is not an option. And though a faux-sabbatical yearlong adventure may mean the nagging career obligation rears its head, don't ask if it's still worth doing. Instead ask, How can I maintain my livelihood while also having an adventure year abroad?

Perhaps you have the good fortune of working for a global company that can transfer you overseas with a sweet expat deal. If so, be grateful you won't have to worry about money or other pesky details. Instead, use your creative energy to tailor your adventure to reflect your family culture instead of your corporate culture. This will be its own challenge. For the vast majority of people, however, getting creative about making *work* work falls into one of the three categories described below.

1. Shape-shift Your Current Job

Whether you go for a full-on sabbatical (suspending your work for a period) or prefer to rearrange your workaday world, the beauty of twenty-first-century life means you don't need to be chained to a desk in an office. With ubiquitous Internet and cheap technology, work today means that, for many professions, one does not have to be present in order to show up.

Have laptop, will travel is enough for some employers (who want happy employees) to offer their workers free rein on where to reside. If you have a skill that can be transmitted via computer, it's easy to share documents online, meet via videoconferencing or phone calls, and collaborate in a variety of ways—time differences notwithstanding.

Other ways to maneuver a shape-shift include working part-time remotely, negotiating infrequent trips back to the office for crucial meetings, or even getting a temporary leave of absence (with or without pay). If your company wants to consider itself progressive and keep its employees happy, encouraging sabbaticals is one way they can shine.

It might be up to you to convince your employer you can stay connected and committed despite being physically absent. But first you might have to convince *yourself.* None of these potential shape-shifts will seem ideal unless you break away from a traditional mindset about your job—and then come up with a construct acceptable to the powers that be.

Moses Jones, a math instructor at Chemeketa Community College in Salem, Oregon, taught classes online for the seven months he was living in his wife's hometown of Verona, Italy. He reduced his normal teaching load and ramped up once he returned to the US. His wife, Rossella Mariotti-Jones, was only able to convince her employer to give her a four-month leave of absence. So she returned home ahead of Moses and their two boys, who were attending school in Verona.

However incomplete their time abroad was, Moses and Rossella achieved their Why: Their sons became fluent in their mom's native language, and they developed stronger ties to their relatives in Italy. All this was accomplished despite the messages they got early on that doing it would be too disruptive for the family.

Plenty of people get creative about how they might work remotely, but it still requires a leap. If the thought of broaching the subject with your boss trips you up, do some research (search terms: negotiate + sabbatical). Consider how you might move forward with the notion of shape-shifting your job (search terms: digital + nomads; work + remotely). Have a sense for what you can bring to the table when presenting the idea, and what you're willing to give up—and also when you're willing to walk away.

2. Completely Shift Your Job

Sometimes, a complete shift is a welcome change—especially if what's calling you to live overseas is the dream of a whole new life. Don't let a dramatic change scare you if that's what bubbles up when you consider your Why. Project forward a decade or so. Then consider that the scary life/career shift coupled with a leap overseas could be a big plot twist in your life story, like it was for these folks.

My sister, Annette, and her then-boyfriend, Toshi, always wanted to live in a foreign country; it didn't matter where. However, they still wanted to build their resumes as architects, which meant they'd need to head to an English-speaking country. So, in 2001, they discovered that Singapore was welcoming foreigners with open arms. They each secured employment with an architecture firm and used their free time to travel throughout Asia. Upon their return to the United States three years later, they found desirable jobs in San Francisco, in part because they stood out from the crowd with their fresh international experience.

Jacqueline Bendy and Stanley Holt, along with their three kids, were determined to spend a year in China. In 2011, Stanley was able to shape-shift his Los Angeles job and work remotely. But Jacqueline, who had just earned her ESL (English as a Second Language) teaching certificate, opted for a whole new career experience. She was hired to teach English to Chinese students at a new school in Shenzhen, China. Their kids were immersed in the local culture, and, like Annette and Toshi, the family used the time abroad to travel extensively.

Le Billington and Jon Joseph hatched a similar radical plan for their family of five. With a burning desire to pull their children, then aged fifteen, eleven, and six, out of the comfortable bubble of American life, Le and Jon both enrolled in an online program to earn their teaching credentials and eventual master's degrees. With bachelor's degrees under their belts already, they spent an intense year and a half completing requirements for their teaching certification, including a state qualifying exam. They knew plenty of schools around the world readily hired teacher-certified native English speakers, many with generous packages appealing to a family.

A first teaching job in Kazakhstan in 2011 sparked their nomadic instincts, prompting a second engagement in Indonesia. It has since become a way of life for the Joseph family. Using joyjobs.com, Le and Jon sourced other opportunities, landing them stints in Istanbul, Turkey, and Lusaka, Zambia, and who knows where to next.

If the idea of a different career path calls you, spend time digging around (search terms: work + overseas; jobs + [pick your country]). You'll get an endless list of websites—that need your vetting, of course—which can start the wheels turning. Even better if you can determine which of your desirable skills will open doors for you, particularly in less advanced countries with greater needs.

Still, a complete shift might mean moving away from your traditional job and toward a true sabbatical. If that's what you're after, track down a copy of *Escape 101* by Dan Clements and Tara Gignac. It offers great insights into viable ways of making a little-to-no-work sabbatical happen. As the authors, who understand the sobering reality of what it takes, say in their book:

> Make no mistake: leaving a career you've invested
> many years in is going to feel like a very big rock to

get moving. If it helps to break it down, you're really looking at three options. The first is to leave your job, and return to it after your hiatus. The second is to leave your job permanently. Since you can always change your mind and choose the second one anytime you please, it usually makes sense best to pursue the first option. The trick is not to choose the third option, which is to never leave.[9]

3. Design-It-Yourself Year

An increasing number of people today fall into the "design-it-yourself" category in terms of livelihood. More laudably put, they are folks with an *entrepreneurial* bent. Some might be small business owners or self-employed consultants. Others may have a bread-and-butter job that pays most or all of the bills, along with a separate passion project or money-making venture, which offers a financial boost.

If this describes you, you won't need to ask a boss or an HR department for permission for personal time off, or even to take a sabbatical. But the freedom from corporate shackles comes with a price. The pressure of maintaining a steady stream of income, health insurance, marketing, and all those pesky details built into the overhead of a bigger company is all on you.

My husband and I fall into this consultant category, and our design-it-yourself plan went like this: We socked away savings for several years leading up to the adventure abroad. We reserved an extra six months' worth of living expenses, knowing that upon our return we'd want to ramp back up without financial pressure.

Since my husband didn't want to cut clients off cold turkey and risk relationship loss, we conceded that some email, conference calls, and video calls would be part of regular life in Italy. However, with intention, he made a drastic reduction in his work load. And because clients knew our year abroad was exceptional, they accepted he'd be incommunicado during our many travel periods.

For those who aren't fully self-employed, design-it-yourself could mean suspending a bread-and-butter job while still finding a way to keep the side income stream going, or even growing. For others who have traditional full-time employment, design-it-yourself might involve quitting a job and then winging it upon your return. You might even sell your house to pay for the trip, intending to buy or rent something else when you get back.

Loey Werking Wells, along with her husband, Andy, and their daughter, Dylan, did just that in order to travel around the world. Andy knew he likely had a job waiting (but no guarantees). Loey, a writer and soon-to-be homeschooler mom, could work from anywhere. They leaped. And the risk was worth it, despite the unexpected time it took to find a house upon their return.

Some brave souls simply let their adventure evolve.

Jen Shafer and her partner, Patrick, figured volunteering for periods would make their travels more affordable, since it covers a good chunk of housing and meals. They ended up liking the cultural immersion and personal rewards of volunteering so much that it became the major theme of their travels for a year. And what a bonus that the cost savings enabled them to stretch their adventure to twenty-four months! Their experience has morphed somewhat into a lifestyle, which you can read about on Jen's blog, SlowlyGlobal.blogspot.com.

A similar DIY family travel adventure began in 2012 for Adam and Emily Harteau, who maintain the blog OurOpenRoad.com. The photographer and writer couple, along with their young daughter, paid for their initial trip—a six-month drive from California to Tierra del Fuego in a camper van—by selling most of their possessions and launching a Kickstarter fund. Fast-forward a few years (with a baby born on the road), and they continue to enjoy the nomadic lifestyle, funded by procuring indigenous works of beauty and selling them online, along with their own creations. This combination of entrepreneurial lifestyle and wing-ing it on the road may not work for everyone, but it's a testament to "where there's a will, there's a way."

The Bottom Line

While we're talking about how to afford your adventure, there is the invisible bottom line of knowing the value of your life choices. For this, we affirm the belief that upending your regular income stream is a reasonable price to pay to have an adventure abroad.

What made it click for my family on a deeper level was some-thing I read about Stefan Sagmeister, a well-known designer and cofounder of the New York design firm Sagmeister & Walsh. He turns the idea of retirement on its head and espouses a different philosophy. Instead of waiting till the end of one's career to retire, he believes life is better served by folding in a sabbatical year every seven years, and retiring a bit later.

As a creative professional, Sagmeister understands well the need to recharge and regenerate ideas. As expressed in his 2009 TED Talk,[10] his sabbaticals are not only a welcome respite; they allow him to enhance his skills and *improve* his work. Ultimately, his sabbaticals *grow* his business. The idea of recharging one's creativity doesn't only belong to designer types. I would argue that life is one giant creative process. And if you can get on board with that, why *wouldn't* you want to figure out a way to make your adventure happen?

Managing Your Money While Abroad

Another aspect of preparing for extended time abroad is figur-ing out how you will access your money while you're out of the country.

The days of travelers' checks are long gone, yet credit card use is not ubiquitous in all other parts of the planet. And neither international banking nor opening a bank account in a foreign country is as straightforward as you might think. So research the specifics for your target country. That said, consider the following as you set yourself up for success during your adventure year.

Credit Cards

Choose them wisely. Credit cards charge a percentage fee for every foreign transaction you make. On top of this, different credit card companies calculate currency exchange at different rates. While the fractional difference may seem negligble, a year's worth of spending can add up.

If you'd rather avoid those fees, then take the time to call the various cards you're considering. On a single weekday, ask each of them what their exact exchange rate is for that date. Then compare and choose. And to state the obvious: have at least one card *without foreign transaction fees*. Even better if it accrues frequent-flier miles.

Also, don't forget to let your credit card companies know which countries you'll be traveling in. The last thing you need is your card rejected right when you're rushing to catch a train or at some other stress-inducing moment.

ATM Fees

Make sure your cash sits in an accessible bank account with minimal to no ATM fees. Since opening a local bank account might not be practical—either because you aren't a citizen of your target country or because you want to avoid possible tax consequences—you will likely be withdrawing cash on a regular basis. And since ATM fees are almost always charged when you use an international bank machine, you want a clear understanding on how your bank back home handles those fees. Some firms in the US (Charles Schwab for one) will reimburse those outside bank fees, in addition to not charging their customers a fee.

The same goes for your home bank's international currency exchange rates. Just like credit card purchases, when you take foreign currency out of a foreign ATM, the exchange rate varies.

You'll want to shop around to make sure your money sits in an account most favorable to *you,* instead of your bank's profits.

Online Banking

Because you'll be paying bills from abroad, you'll want to ensure that your online banking is up to date with any and all payees. And for anything else that requires regular payment, you'll want to switch to paperless online billing if you haven't already.

To make sure nothing falls through the cracks while you're away, I suggest creating a spreadsheet with your typical monthly payments and any regular but less-frequent bills you can think of, such as annual life insurance premiums. Scour the previous couple of years of transactions to be thorough. Then set up auto-pay for any payees where it makes sense to do so. Your aim is to avoid unnecessary time spent paying bills, while minimizing any negative hit to your credit rating by forgetting to pay them!

Everyday Transactions

As you research your target country, you'll want to get a sense for how everyday transactions work. For example, we were surprised at how much of a cash culture Italy still was in 2014. We even paid our rent in cash. Knowing that in advance meant we didn't need to open a local bank account, which would have been its own set of hassles. We could cover everything with regular ATM withdrawals and a credit card.

Ask around in your ambassador resource circles how other expats in your target location manage their daily financial activities. Though you may get conflicting answers, you'll be better informed on how to plan your access to money.

ℓℓ

All this research regarding banking and credit card fees might feel like you're following a bouncing ball, since rules often change.

Adding to the jumble is the likelihood of getting a different answer depending on whom you talk to. So take notes and take down names! In the event you need to contest a fee, having specifics at the ready will increase the odds that a company will keep you, their customer, happy at the end of the day.

HOUSING

One of the trickiest things about relocating for only a year is housing. That includes not only finding a temporary residence abroad but also figuring out what to do with your house back home. It would be naïve to think that solving for both of these challenges will happen in an easy, linear fashion. So, prepare to feel like you're doing a delicate tightrope walk, especially if you are also applying for a visa. To curtail the stress, let's take a closer look at each end of the housing issue with an eye toward a simple strategy.

Finding Move-In Ready Housing Abroad

If you're like most adults I know, you've moved more than a few times in your life. You know the drill of renting an apartment: Move to a new town; stay with friends or find temporary housing; parade through a dozen or so options until they become a blur; choose one with fingers crossed, then sign on the dotted line.

Moving halfway around the planet for a year can be trickier. You could follow the familiar rent-an-apartment routine, though ideally you'll want a place that's already furnished and includes utilities. You might also require a place convenient to school or public transportation. Such must-haves mean a drastic reduction in choices, unless perhaps you're heading to a top tourist spot (in which case, expect higher rent).

It may cross your mind to search *all* housing options, *including* unfurnished, assuming that furnishing it on the cheap once you're there will be easy. Perhaps that's doable if you'll have an Ikea or similar nearby. But make no mistake, you won't want to spend the time (or money) to set up a home with furniture, appliances, kitchenware, etc. when you will be there for a relatively short period. And that's not even considering the headache of clearing out your flat before you return to your homeland.

So let's dive in with some big-picture tips for finding housing as you pull together your adventure without pulling out your hair.

Learn the Lay of the Land

First, give a nod of gratitude that we live with twenty-first-century technology that makes this process much easier than it used to be. Then create a Google map for the area you're targeting. Mark the spots you hope to be near (school, bus stop, etc.), because for any kind of daily commute, a reasonable distance will pay huge dividends. Then review your map whenever you see references to streets and areas in your online forums or lodging descriptions. You'll begin to absorb a mental image of your target location, which will make your research easier.

Search the Heck out of Vacation Rental Sites...

...for they are the motherlode of furnished apartments. Airbnb, VRBO, and booking.com are the big ones at the moment, but many others are elbowing into the marketplace, though they vary in popularity, depending on the region. The listings pertain to short-term travel, making them perfect for those planning a 'round-the-world adventure. But there are plenty of owners who would welcome a long-term inquiry. Imagine, for them, a whole year of not having to deal with multiple guests, ins and outs, cleanings, etc. So if you discover a listing that isn't booked out far into the future, in all likelihood you'll be able to negotiate a significant reduction from the price that's displayed.

Even if a vacation listing ends up being unavailable, don't lose heart. A warm exchange with the owner could prove fruitful on *any* front, including giving you the heads-up on other rental properties that aren't (yet) listed online.

Work Your (Growing) Network

This goes without saying, but any contacts in your target location might know someone (who might know someone) who has a property for rent. As you research and reach out in your school search, for example, ask about housing. Often, someone knows of a flat being prepared for future rentals, and locals have their own insider resources for furnishing a place—something impossible to pull together from afar. Also ask your contacts if they know of any rental agencies. A local rental agency might present you with the best options. But be forewarned that hefty fees may apply, so know what you're getting into.

The network in your destination town may hold a potential set of eyes and ears should you find a prospective winner online. Nothing beats stepping into a place, or trying before you buy. But barring that, the next best thing is having someone else be your stand-in.

Consider that Reconnaissance Trip

If you can swing it, fly out and see places firsthand. It may seem intimidating, or a needless expense, especially if your visa hasn't been approved yet. But you could look at it this way: Every connection you forge in your home-to-be will make it that much easier to integrate once you're there. A more close-up inspection of dwelling options might help you avoid unpleasant surprises like building quirks, sketchy neighborhoods, or difficult landlords.

Sneak in a reconnaissance trip even if timing it is a challenge (think of those frequent-flier miles!). You could do it far in advance to get a real leg up on knowing the town, build your network, and even check out potential properties. Conversely, a brief trip close to your arrival date will give you a more realistic picture of housing choices if that is your sole purpose for reconnaissance.

And consider this: A property owner who meets you in person could be intrigued by the upside of renting to a first-world foreigner who only plans to stay a year. Put bluntly, they won't have to worry about you becoming a squatter, and they might look forward to charging a higher rent after you leave.

Adjust Your Expectations

It's entirely possible you will land a dream house at a reasonable cost for your year abroad. It is equally possible that your dwelling mode will make a dramatic shift toward basic—if for no other reason than the vast majority of the world lives a more modest lifestyle than Americans. A bedroom for each kid? Don't count on it. A home office? If you're lucky or able to increase your budget. Closets with space? A big fat maybe. A spacious kitchen with all the tools you're used to having? Forget it.

Beyond size and furnishings, prepare for the dearth of reliable Wi-Fi, washer/dryers, and cheap gas and electricity. This is when you return to your essential Why. If your answer is solid, then it won't matter whether you are camping or living in a castle.

I might add that while living in a castle sounds seductive, it doesn't equate to a better or more successful year abroad. When you live more like the average Joe in your target destination, you increase your accessibility and relatability, which increases the odds of building genuine relationships with locals. Your year abroad memories are made of those relationships. Besides, the best growth happens when you are out of your comfort zone—and not cocooning in luxury.

Note for 'Round-the-World Travelers

The house-hunting aspect of your journey will be much easier than it is for those seeking a single home for twelve months. You'll find an abundance of temporary tourist housing online for most places you're planning to visit.

Because you'll be on the move, the short stints at each locale also mean that pulling the trigger on a flat isn't such a big deal. If it sucks, just check out. You can rent by the week, day, or month and move on.

Also, if you don't plan to stay in any one place too long, you won't need to show proof of housing in order to obtain a long-term visa. While traipsing around the planet may take its energetic toll, the freedom to change your surroundings on a whim can be quite liberating.

About Your House Back Home

Unless you aim to untether yourself completely and leave all possible futures on the table, you will transition back to some semblance of your current life in your current house. To be sure, there are those who have sold their homes to *fund* their adventures abroad, and others who use the transition back as an opportunity to relocate. But the majority of temporary adventurers abroad need to figure out what to do with their house back home while they are away.

Do You Ditch It?

If you rent your current home, and for whatever reason can't or don't want to sublease it, then you only have one to-do: Move out. You'll have deal with your stuff (sell it or store it), but after that you'll be free as a bird. This is an elegant scenario if you hope to make a major life change after you return.

Or perhaps you own your home but want a clean break. Selling it and starting clean is an option, but be prepared: The stress you would save on the launch end of your year abroad by *not* renting out your place could come back to haunt you.

This happened to Loey Werking Wells and her family, who had thought the simplest thing to enable their year of travel was to sell their house and invest in a new one once they returned. But they hadn't anticipated a tight market, higher costs, and a fourteen-month delay in getting resettled in a new home. While there are countless factors you can't predict, one is irrefutable: Moving is a ginormous hassle. So consider with care whether you think you'll be willing to tackle a house hunt and a move after returning from a year abroad.

Or Rent It Out?

Like many who move locations temporarily, we rented out our house for the year to help cover costs both here *and* abroad. Some lucky folks who live in competitive rental markets manage to cover the lion's share of their adventure simply because they have a low or paid-off mortgage. By charging the standard market rates, they bring in significant rental income. On the flip side, those who live in a lackluster market could be begging a house sitter to take care of their place. A little housing market research will inform your best approach.

What About a House Swap?

I would be remiss if I didn't bring up the enticing scenario that could solve both the "find housing there" *and* the "what to do with my house here" problems: a house swap.

If you live in a university town or other type of go-to locale, it could be worth your while to explore the possibility of exchanging houses with another family (search terms: home or house + exchange or swap + sabbatical). This ideal-sounding scenario requires tremendous flexibility on your part in terms of timing and location—*if* you even find a potential swap, that is.

✤

If, after considering the above options, you're determined to keep one of your biggest assets intact, renting your house is a no-brainer. If you go this route, these are the basic points of consideration:

Rent It Furnished or Unfurnished?

Odds are, you will rent your house to people you don't know, in which case you must decide whether you're comfortable with others using all your stuff. It's easiest and most cost-effective to rent your furnished home. You won't have to hassle with movers or a truck, and you won't have to pay to store your furniture. You'll *still* do plenty of culling and clearing out before your departure, which can be a plus. And you'll need to make sure your stuff is in decent enough shape for a renter. So "easy" is relative, I suppose.

Renting your house furnished also means securing your valuables and personal items. That might involve lugging them to the basement, the attic, or an extra room where you can lock them up. Or perhaps a friend will loan you space in their house. And if you end up paying a storage locker fee for your personal items, it will be far cheaper than hauling all your furniture and belongings out (and back again) for the entire year. But prepare for either scenario.

It's possible you'll only find folks willing to rent an empty house. Remember the phrase "everything is a trade-off." Your house as a furnished rental means an entire year of wear and tear on your stuff. Your empty house as a rental means clearing it out. So, you'll either be practicing nonattachment or spending the money and energy to lock up your valuables.

Hire an Agency, Manager, or Helper

When you are halfway across the globe, bottom at the list of things you want to do is manage the rental of your house. Who wants to deal with a broken sewer pipe back home while you are 9,000 miles away basking on a beach in Goa? So, consider your options:

- Hire a management company, which typically takes a percentage of the rent, plus other unexpected fees that come up (such as that broken sewer pipe).

- Pay a trusted individual to be on call in case issues arise, which may involve a small retainer fee plus an hourly rate.
- Rely on a friend or family member who loves you unconditionally and with whom you don't mind accruing interest in the obligation bank.

Management companies tend to be full-service. They screen tenants, collect rent, and use their experience and resources to handle any problems that arise, letting you live your life beyond the border. Should you take this route, follow due diligence and ask for references on any rental company. At a minimum, read Yelp or Angie's List reviews with somewhat of a skeptical eye. Using a trusted friend, contact, or family member will probably cost you a fair amount less, and may or may not be equally worry-free.

Keep It Legal and Cover Your Assets

No matter what you end up doing, a formalized agreement with tenants is in order. You can find a standard lease online, and you'll want to make sure it covers the points pertinent to your situation (for example, pets, pool, etc.).

Other details easy to overlook: getting formal consent from your mortgage company that allows you to legally rent, and adjusting your homeowner's insurance so it's valid for renting. Mere technicalities, but the last thing you want is for something to happen while you're gone, only to find out your insurance won't pay because you had renters living there.

Safeguarding the largest asset you own can be a bit of a hassle, but it allows you peace of mind while you're away. And coming back to a cozy, familiar home is a welcome event after a year of unpredictability in a foreign land.

It's Not Just the House

As you read through this chapter and scan the broad array of things to manage in order to realize your dream, you'll start to get why I equate going abroad for a year with climbing a mountain. You essentially move twice in twelve months. And moving is one of those top life stressors like getting married or having a child. It's a big deal that takes up a lot of energy.

Instead of moving, perhaps it's more manageable to think of this huge undertaking as "suspending" your current life. While we all have a different variety of administrative tasks in our lives, mundane or otherwise, here are the biggies to check off to allow for an unencumbered year away:

Access to Important Documents

Among the valuables you'll lock up for the year may be documents you'll need to access. These could be anything from tax returns to health care records, such as recent test results. Or even birth certificates, as we learned.

When officials in Genoa informed us that the Italian Consulate in San Francisco mistakenly granted our children the wrong visa, we were told to get certified translated birth certificates for our daughters. Good thing we remembered where we had locked them up and a friend was able to ship them to us. But it would have been a major hassle if they had been buried somewhere in storage. Moral of the story: If it's possible you'll need it—for tax filing, travel, visa, etc.—make sure a trusted person will have access.

Club Memberships and Subscriptions

It's a safe assumption you won't be shopping at Costco while you're exploring a new corner of the globe, so do you really want to pay its annual fee? And do you fancy paying international magazine subscription fees when online content is plentiful? Suspending memberships and subscriptions is easy. And once you return home you can pick up where you left off—if you want to, that is.

Spend a couple of hours compiling a list and making phone calls so you feel the satisfaction of checking this one off your list.

Mail Forwarding

If you plan to travel continuously, you won't have a stable address where you can receive mail. And even if you move overseas to a single location, you may not want to rely on mail forwarding. Transferring to an international address is not straightforward, and any packages you receive will have to go through customs.

Still, it's tempting to find a way to make basic USPS mail forwarding work for you. The beauty of being away for a single year is in your favor. It means you can take advantage of the service without needing to inform a slew of businesses of any address change. You simply cancel the forwarding service when you return home, and the postal carrier recommences mail delivery at your home address. A bonus might even be that solicitations and unwanted catalogs will drop you from their lists. But the question of what address you forward to remains.

For a fee, companies (search terms: mail + forwarding + service) will manage this for you by letting you forward to their address. The service involves scanning your mail and forwarding (or not) per your instructions.

Another option is to ask a trusted friend or family member to be your mail forwarding service, alerting you to anything that seems important. Your main goal: Don't let any item that needs your attention fall through the cracks.

Utilities

If you have renters in your home, utility bills will get transferred in name to them. Otherwise, inquire with your utility companies on how best to suspend billing while you're away. Some might require you to close an account and reopen it upon your return.

Taxes

When you leave the country for a year, it doesn't mean you can forget about ol' Uncle Sam. You still must file taxes from abroad, even when you don't have an income. This may not be true for state income, as that rule varies by state. Also, you may qualify for a foreign earned income exclusion if you are earning money in another country. All the variation on rules and statutes means you should sit down with your accountant or CPA, who hopefully has some experience with other clients who've lived abroad.

Telephone

If you prefer folks back home to have seamless access to you, bring your cell phone and convert it to an international plan. You can also transform your current landline number to a VoIP (Voice over Internet Protocol) phone, often done through your Internet service provider or a popular service such as Vonage. Then, wherever you have an Internet connection, people can call the number they're used to calling without incurring long-distance charges. Either scenario won't negate your need to have a local cell phone wherever you end up living, however.

On the other hand, if you don't want to receive phone calls as usual, simply leave a voice mail announcing that you will not be reachable except for emergencies. You can always let people know how to contact you via another channel of communication.

Your Car

Will you sell it? Loan it out? Let it sit? Whatever you decide, look into insurance. There is no need for you to pay the full amount if it sits in the garage. And likewise, if you loan it to someone else, you'll want to make sure *they* are covered for the year instead of you.

Your Unique Needs

As you build your to-do list within these categories and others (more on organizing that list later in this chapter), make note of anything else that might need oversight while you're away. As the list grows, think about which projects and obligations you can extract yourself from before you go and what you can put off until you get back. For example, if you sit on any work, school, or nonprofit committees that have ongoing or long-term goals, consider disengaging well before your departure. But if there's an obligation that requires your consistent attention—say, a community garden plot or a business entity you manage— then you'll need to come up with a plan to delegate.

ℓℓ

All of the administrative issues involving your house, bills, personal papers, and such call for you to strike a balance while you're away. It's the balance between needing to keep a hand on the steering wheel and blissful noninvolvement, which can be challenging. We opted to hire someone to manage our home world while we were away.

Sarah, who had worked as our occasional nanny and home office assistant, fell under the category of family without the shared DNA. She was the perfect person to act as our surrogate when any issues arose. We created a separate bank account and made her co-signatory. Then, if a house-related problem or an unexpected bill not payable online cropped up, we could transfer enough funds for her to cut a check and deal with it. She also let us use her address for mail forwarding and informed us when anything noteworthy arrived.

Sarah was our perfect solution. Perhaps you can identify a Sarah in your life, too.

SCHOOLS AND EDUCATION

Options for Your Kids

The single most important choice for your children will be their schooling. A successful learning adventure abroad will depend on how connected they are to the experience once your year gets under way. If they're happy, you'll be happy; if they're miserable, get ready for a torturous year.

In preparation for your year abroad, if you want your child to return to his or her current school, it's best to get reassurance from your principal. If your children are enrolled in a standard neighborhood public school, this should be a non-issue. But if they're in a specialized or lottery public school, it might take some behind-the-scenes dealing to garner a promise of a return.

If your children attend a private school, it'll be at the discretion of the director how simple their reentry will be. You might be asked to pay full or partial tuition while you're away.

In any scenario—private or public—if you've been an active and involved family, the school should want you back. In a perfect world they will see the value of your child's return after an eye-opening year abroad. But don't leave your children's education to chance by making assumptions. Have an idea of what your ideal scenario is upon your return, and prepare accordingly.

In looking forward to that eye-opening year abroad, figuring out the education component for your children is a big piece of the puzzle. Like every other decision you make, you'll face trade-offs during this outside-of-the-box year with outside-of-the-box-academics. Once you determine your destination, your schooling options are pretty straightforward and will fall into some combination of these three categories:

1. International School

These private schools of varying cost (often not cheap) are pretty much guaranteed to have a curriculum in English. Usually located in large urban areas or capital cities, they tend to cater to an international student body with a heavy expat population. But local families who want to ensure English fluency for their kids pursue international schools too. These schools may go by various names (such as American or British School) but aren't to be confused with an English school, whose primary aim is to teach English as a second language.

Potential upsides:

- Curriculum is often International Baccalaureate or a similar high standard, designed to be transfer-friendly. This makes for an easier transition back home with minimal concern that your child will fall behind their grade level.
- Since the curriculum is in English, there won't be any language challenges to cause the concern that things aren't sinking in.
- Forming friendships will be easier, due to sharing either a common language or a similar expat experience.

Potential downsides:

- Lack of full foreign-language immersion. If you're heading to a non-English-speaking country for a year and hoping for a new language acquisition, it likely won't happen if you send your kids to an English-language international school.
- Compromised cultural immersion. Since English is the primary language, and there are likely to be other expat families at the school, chances are greater that your child will click with non-natives, minimizing friendships with the locals. Similarly, if your child's school is *your* main connection to the local community,

it means your friendships will more than likely be struck from this same expat pool.

- Transient vibe. Since international schools tend to be popular with expat families, who are often living abroad for a few years at a time, they may have more of a passing-through quality. This is compounded by the fact that kids will come from many different neighborhoods to attend the school.

2. Local School

If your aim is a full cultural and language immersion, you'll be looking at the probable option of a local public school. I say *probable* because some countries require language proficiency, or they may shunt your kid over to a school set up for non-native speakers, which would defeat the goal of full cultural immersion.

Wherever you choose to live, the reputation of a country's educational system will vary. Public schools in Scandinavia are the envy of the global community. But around much of the planet, schools are overcrowded and offer limited resources. Even in the US, this is sadly the case, so it might not be *that* different from what you're used to.

If you aren't thrilled about the public school options where you're headed, there may be affordable private options that don't fall under the aforementioned international school category. Often they are *parochial* schools that exist under the aegis of a religious institution, so be prepared for that.

Depending on where you'll live, you might experience a religious overtone in your local public school. For example, our girls attended a public school in Italy where crucifixes on the wall and weekly religion class were par for the course. We accepted it as part of the cultural experience, and our heathen children are no worse for it.

Potential upsides:

- Language acquisition, assuming you head to a non-English-speaking land. There is no better or faster way for kids to learn another language than by full immersion and mingling with their peers. Be patient, though, as it can take three to five months for the language to click and a sense of ease to set in.
- Full cultural immersion. Enrollment in a local school is your fast track to becoming part of the local community. You will experience the best of the culture *and* get a taste for its problems firsthand.

Potential downsides:

- Making friends with classmates may be more of a challenge, especially at first. Patience is required!
- Academics may not align with your child's school once you return. Your kids might need to play catch-up, even for subjects omitted (for example, your homeland history will be replaced with local history).

3. Homeschooling

If the bulk of your year abroad consists of meandering around the world, you will be homeschooling. Also, if for any reason you aren't comfortable sending your kids to local schools, you will homeschool—*provided it's a legal option where you're headed.*

Homeschooling requires you to map out the subjects you hope to cover and pace out lessons with your children. You can acquire a preset curriculum for this (search: homeschool + curriculum), which makes it much easier. You might explore enrolling in an online school (search: online schools + expats), which will impose even more structure.

A more radical version of schooling at home is called *unschooling*. Child-led unschooling leaves the parent out of the equation unless the child asks to learn about something in particular.
Potential upsides:

- Freedom from routine. You can organize your days entirely around your whims. If you want to travel, there's no need to navigate around a school schedule.
- The world can be your learning environment. You can incorporate your travels and surroundings into lessons, making them memorable.

Potential downsides:

- You will take on the role of teacher or, at a minimum, "time management overseer." This could prove challenging for your kids as well as for you—especially if you're used to getting that chunk of time for yourself when they're at school. It's a commitment not to be underestimated.
- If you become lax with homeschooling, you might pay the price in panic down the road should your child expect to reenter his or her previous school on par with classmates.

No matter which path you choose for your child, you can't research it enough. Expat boards for your target country are a great start. Another way to gather details or even connect with other parents is via Facebook pages for various schools in your intended community, and homeschoolers around the world.

Whether or not you speak the language of your destination country, you'll be able to glean specifics about your local school options. You can let auto translation do its thing on the web. Or post a translated query in a forum or page, which could yield a handful of useful replies needed to help you evaluate a school.

If you're worried about feeling like a fish out of water in a local non-English-based school, don't let that stop you from at least exploring the option. Local school communities in countries where English is not the official language are near certain to consider it a boon when native English speakers enroll.

As always, keep in mind that any connections you make during your school research phase might prove invaluable as you navigate other aspects of your climb up the year abroad mountain. Ambassadors can appear at any stage of your preparation.

And remember, nothing is written in stone. Plenty of people switch things up once they get settled. Bridget and Kevin Kresse decided to pull their adolescent twins out of a questionable classroom midway through the year and homeschool for a while. In his book *A Family Year Abroad,* Chris Westphal tells how his family loved their international school, but they couldn't tolerate the hour-plus commute (in a taxicab, no less). So they broke their apartment lease and moved closer to the school. Like anything in life, make your best choice and go from there.

What About Cultural Immersion for Younger Children?

Even though younger children don't attend school, parents might benefit from a routine or occasional break during their adventurous year abroad. When seeking childcare such as day care or preschool, two basic steps apply anywhere:

1. Ask around. Whether you're looking for a day care center for regular part-time coverage or a babysitter, call upon the folks in your network. A personal

reference—even from a friend of a friend—can provide peace of mind. You should also get a sense for the going rate and/or how the system works in whatever culture you're immersed in.

2. Visit with and interview potential caregivers. No doubt you'll want to meet in person anyone who will care for your child. If there's a language barrier, bring a translator to ensure you have all your questions answered. Personally, I wouldn't make English fluency a deal-breaker because your younger child will readily learn the caregiver's language.

One area to focus your attention is in understanding cultural differences. Don't make the assumption that your values and norms will fully align with the caregivers you meet. For example, in my family's American social circles, kids under age ten typically go to bed by eight p.m. Imagine our surprise when we arrived in Italy to see toddlers and their families running around the local piazza at eleven p.m.!

The more you can remain curious about the differences and embrace them as part of the adventure, the less discord you'll suffer. Of course, you won't do anything that seems off—but just remember that you signed up for the adventure as a way of breaking up your routine. So expect to break up your routine.

Other areas where cultural norms may differ include teething, potty training, naps, meal time, diet, clothing, child-adult dynamics, gender roles and expectations, and more. So if you have any areas of concern, have your questions ready—particularly if you don't do well with surprises.

Not Just for Kids: Language Schools

Will you need or want a basic proficiency in another language? If the answer is yes, read on. And if you are headed to a place where the official business language is English, accept that you'll miss out if you don't learn the local parlance, which is what summed up these expat experiences.

My sister Annette, the architect we met a few chapters back, spent three years in Singapore, where English is an official language but where all the natives speak Malay or Mandarin. While she learned some local Sing jargon, her one regret about her time in Singapore was that she didn't put any time into basic Mandarin lessons.

Similarly, Stuart Brown and Michelle Radford-Brown, who spent a few years in Amsterdam, where English is ubiquitous, reported that they were effectively kept at the outskirts of the local social scene. They were relegated to the world of expats because they did not speak any Dutch.

So unless you aim for the United Kingdom, Australia, or a handful of other countries, you will probably face the challenge of a local language, even if you're able to get by with English.

ℓℓℓ

If English is *not* a major language in your target country, what's your best tactic to prepare for the year? If you already have familiarity and ability with the target foreign language, once there you'll be past the sink-or-swim stage. Your vocabulary and ease with communicating will improve daily—even though at times it will feel like you take three steps forward and two steps back.

But what if you're a practical virgin to your target language and still want to arrive with a modicum of skill? You'll juggle plenty in the months leading up to your departure, and adding "learn another language" to the list might put you over the edge. Don't despair! Whatever you can manage will benefit you.

Our efforts to learn Italian included purchasing Rosetta Stone, a popular computer and online course. I think my husband used it a dozen times—at most—in the six months before we left for Italy; the girls managed it a little more regularly. I can't say that we squeezed out our money's worth, but it did increase our comfort and familiarity with the language.

And while I myself had studied Italian for twenty-five years, and am more or less fluent, being thrown into the deep end of the pool once we landed still had my brain sweating in almost every conversation. A new accent, local verbiage, and high-velocity chatter made me painfully aware that even a whole year in Italy would only get me so far with my second language.

Practical Tips for Language Learning Before Departure

- **Study up on your own time.** Purchase a program, especially if you're a beginner. (Fewer programs exist for advanced students.) If you don't want to shell out money, it's a safe bet your local library has several options—including physical materials for borrowing as well as access to online programs.
- **Hire a native speaker, preferably with teaching experience, to give you and your family lessons.** If no one in your community comes recommended, seek someone out online through any number of established programs (search terms: [X foreign language] + teacher + online). Regular lessons keep you accountable and less likely to procrastinate. Figure out what works best for you and run with it.
- **Sign up for classes at a local college or language school.** In-person classes offer the advantage of meeting people who might be able to introduce you to contacts in your destination country. (Remember those ambassadors!) Also, finding a language practice buddy is a sure way to increase proficiency.
- **Research language schools in your target location.** When you know your target town, explore possibilities

for lessons once you arrive. Not only does this let you hit the ground running, but connecting with locals in advance of your arrival can prove extremely useful. For example, people who work at language schools are likely to have several housing contacts at their fingertips. (If you aren't sure exactly where you'll be living, finding language schools in various possible target destinations might help you narrow the field, or even nail down a spot.)

While it won't be crucial to register for classes in advance (unless your visa requires it), just doing the research will familiarize you to your new world abroad, laying the foundation for a successful transition.

GETTING A VISA

Unless you know people in just the right places, or already hold citizenship in your target country, prepare to run the gauntlet of getting a visa. This can be a stressful process. And it makes climbing your mountain—often in the dark—all the more challenging, given that you're also seeking housing, renting your current house, sorting your finances, and so on.

While we've heard stories of people who have moved abroad without bothering to get legal permission, I don't recommend such a clandestine lifestyle. Still, obtaining a valid visa for wherever you plan to live can be an onerous task. But it's arguably less stressful than facing authorities who ask for papers you don't have.

As much as I advocate being a global citizen and can imagine, à la John Lennon, a world without countries (nor the wars fought over them), we live on a planet with tighter borders and increasing surveillance. With that come electronic passports, stricter visa requirements, and heightened security measures. In today's world, don't count on being able to slip across a border unnoticed.

The tricky thing is that visa rules vary greatly. Some countries *want* foreigners, along with the influx of money they bring. So they make it easier to enter and stay. Others make it difficult to understand the process to remain legally or to know if you're eligible for an extended stay. Regardless, the rules and requirements vary from nation to nation, visa type to visa type—or even from consulate office to consulate office for the same country (search terms: consulate or "foreign embassy" + [target country] + visas).

Adding to the confusion, each administrator within a single office might interpret or translate the documentation differently. During the visa application process, it's best to accept that it may not follow a logical order. This will help keep your frustrations in check, and maybe set you up to be pleasantly surprised.

The Chicken-and-Egg Dance

The entirety of planning a year abroad presupposes that in the end you're free to go, with permit in hand. Most likely, you'll prepare for your year—find housing and school, figure out how to suspend your life back home, etc.—long before you're even able to apply for an extended stay. In our case, we didn't get our visa documents in the mail until several weeks before our departure. And, ironically, to get approved for the visa, we had to have our plane tickets, health insurance, and even housing—all set to go.

It would be impossible to offer a detailed, step-by-step visa acquisition plan—since everyone's situation, goals, and options are so different. But I hope to ease some of your angst with a few simple directives about how to begin. And if, like me, you're not comfortable in the unknown, preferring instead to have a clear sense of where you stand and how to proceed, then I encourage you to find your zen mind.

Determine Your Best Visa Option

As soon as you decide where you want to live for the year, your top priority is to understand the visa options for that country.

After you scan your target nation's website, you may delight at your array of choices based on terms such as student visa, family visa, resident visa, and so on. But once you drill down and read detailed descriptions, your fitting options become clearer.

You may wonder whether a student visa means full-time student at a university, or if having cousins in said country count as family, or whether self-employment qualifies for a work-related visa. In a perfect world, there's a thorough and clear FAQ on your target country's official website. Otherwise, you must seek clarity.

Consider this: If you end up needing to call a foreign consulate, you might get the inside scoop if an expat friend from your target country does the talking for you. Just having that friend's compatriot connection, and a native language in common, could yield better results for you.

During the most stressful points of our visa application process, I could not get a clear sense of what the Italian consulate was expecting to see in terms of our bank statements. Was there a per-person minimum amount they were looking for? We had no idea how we were supposed to convey our financial picture without feeling completely vulnerable. Then Ale came to the rescue. No stranger to the Italian Consulate and its muddy bureaucracy, she picked up the phone and managed to extract the lowdown from her fellow citizen. That simple, quick phone call took a big edge off our stress.

Explore the Dual-Citizenship Route

It may be easy to get permission to stay in your desired location beyond the typical tourism period. Or it may seem impossible. A lucky small minority of folks can "collect their $200 and pass Go" simply because they qualify for citizenship in a particular country. And even if it's not their target country, thanks to residency agreements and reciprocities, it still might be of benefit.

For example, in the European Union, citizens of one EU country can live and work in another EU country with ease. Thus, if you qualify for Irish dual citizenship by way of a grandparent being born in Ireland, then you could become an Irish citizen but live in France for the year.

If there's a chance you might qualify for dual citizenship, it's worth exploring. You may only need to begin the process in order to qualify for your extended stay. And while jumping through the hoops to gain citizenship might be an added hassle, don't underestimate the payoffs. It could offer you a more integrated experience and an easier transition, and make future stays a piece of cake.

Three Essential Rules for Obtaining Your Visa

1. Find Your Go-To Information Hubs

Whether you go for a regular visa or a less common dual citizenship, prepare for a multistep process involving a lot of red tape. Identifying reliable sources of up-to-date information and people willing to share their experience is key. Perhaps you'll subscribe to a free or fee-based expat website, or follow a few different expat forums, groups, or pages for your target country.

Once you've done your due diligence and feel comfortable with your go-to forums, scour them regularly to find out how the approval process works. Post your questions. Compare responses. As you gather the required documents for your particular visa, each step will probably bring up additional questions (for you and anyone in the forum applying for the same permit). In the spirit of good karma mentioned before: sharing helpful information prompts others to do the same.

A word about these online forums, though…

At times it can be like entering a dark, thorny forest. You'll find a lot of anxious people, and horror stories to boot. You'll recognize repeat responders, many of them helpful—and some not so much. You might notice trolls—expats living in your desired destination who guard their adopted homeland with vigilance.

They often have an agenda (subconscious or otherwise) to keep more expats from entering.

Your job is to walk the fine line of seeking and sharing information without getting caught up in the maelstrom of negative energy. And don't take everything you read as gospel truth. Rather, use it to formulate further questions until you're satisfied the replies are accurate. In the end, it might mean calling the consulate for confirmation—and even then, it might not be accurate to the letter of the law!

Also keep in mind that people can be reluctant to share personal details in online forums. They may be understandably skittish about posting sensitive information regarding income or earnings. Or if someone discovered a loophole in the rules, they may not want to announce it for fear of ruining a good thing. Try to read between the lines and to word questions that avoid asking for specifics. This skill could garner you enough information to gain the next foothold up the mountain.

2. Follow—and Interpret—the *Current* Rules

While following the rules should be straightforward enough, it isn't always clear what they mean. Some things, like getting a certain vaccine, are obvious. But requirements such as proof of income or secured housing can fall into a gray area.

For most of the minor details, your go-to resources will offer precise answers to your questions. But in other cases it might serve you better to submit your application based on your own interpretation—and let consulate officials request a correction from you if they deem it necessary.

Let's take "proof of adequate means" as an example. Officials will no doubt require bank statements to confirm you have enough money to live for the year without state assistance. It's easy to determine how many monthly statements they want, even though a specific dollar amount is an elusive figure. But what if your most adequate bank statements come from an account shared with a person not applying for the visa? It would be foolish to raise the question, "Is it okay if my rich uncle's name is on our bank account?" That could open a can of worms, calling for additional documents you're unable to produce. Sometimes it's better to present your best application—neat, pretty, and organized—and hope you pass muster.

Another point of interpretation might be whether you can work in your target country. A permit might be more obtainable if you won't need a job while living abroad, and therefore won't be taking employment from a native. Does this mean you can't work remotely for a company in your home country?

The remote-work topic was hotly debated in the forums when we were putting together our visa application for Italy. Since no one had a definitive answer, we chose to interpret for ourselves. To us, the rule meant we would not take employment from Italian citizens. We still produced the required paperwork, but we certainly didn't seek clarity on that specific point. We rationalized that Italy was going to get a twelve-month cash infusion from us, without having to provide us all the state benefits.

Navigating the gray areas can be stressful, often with no easy answers or linear pathway through the forest. The best way forward is to keep a steady eye on the goal. And as for the importance of following the *current* rules, let me tell you a story about laws that change.

I met Linda online in one of the expat forums I followed during our visa application process. She had decided to move her family to Malta for a year. It seemed like a brilliant choice: a charming Mediterranean country with English as an official language. They rented out their house in the States and found a school in Malta for their kids after getting all their legal documentation in order.

Or so they thought…

Linda and her husband had gotten a jump on compiling their visa requirements, based on the laws in effect several months before they arrived. But once they settled into Maltese life while completing the process to make their stay official, they received the rude awakening that the laws had changed! It would be difficult and cost-prohibitive to stick with their original plan. So… adventure aborted.

I tell you this story only as a caveat to keep apprised of current law to minimize the chances of this happening to you. (More about having a plan B in the next chapter.) So check the dates on any threads you're following to make sure the information isn't stale.

3. Get Your Best Smile On

If all this navigating isn't stressful enough, dealing with government officials can put you over the edge— especially when they hold the ticket to your dreams. And you could be in frequent and ongoing communication with them. You might even need to travel a significant distance to your designated consul's office, more than once, to meet with officials face to face.

Then again, you might have a perfunctory, nonexistent relationship with your consulate officers. There's no way of predicting. But whatever the case, don't be surprised if the government worker stereotype comes into play. You know the one—where an underpaid paper pusher enjoys holding onto any shreds of power they can wield. No matter the personalities you encounter, kill 'em with kindness, exude politeness, and lose any sense of American entitlement you might harbor deep within.

Bridget Kresse recalls her experience with Manuela when putting together her family's Italian visa application in 2010. Manuela was not at all the warm and fuzzy type. But Bridget, determined to break through, always offered her a friendly, warm demeanor. She never failed to ask Manuela how *she* was doing. And she would remember any personal details Manuela mentioned so she could refer to them in future exchanges. This allowed them to develop a more intimate connection. And no matter the question, Bridget replied with a version of, "Whatever you need, Manuela—just tell us what you need and we'll put it together for you."

Over time Manuela melted a bit, and Bridget felt like they had a rapport. By the end of the application process, Manuela *wanted* the Kresses to get approved. Short of any palm greasing—which is *not at all* what I'm suggesting here—if you create a subtle connection, it will be one more thing in your favor.

This points to that "put good energy out, get good energy back" mantra. Though living such a philosophy won't guarantee you a visa, it *will* reduce your stress, which can run high when all your plans hinge upon getting this ticket abroad.

Visas for 'Round-the-World Travelers

If you hit a rough patch during your visa application process to a single country, the thorniness of it might tempt you to ditch your plans and go for a 'round-the-world adventure instead. We had those moments of wanting to forget about proving our worthiness to Italy and surrender to a rambling adventure with ever-changing scenery. But such a scenario doesn't let you sidestep the stress of planning.

With a 'round-the-world plan, you won't have to worry about a single-issue visa allowing you to extend beyond a nation's normal tourism period. But many countries require a visa for simple travel, regardless of the length of stay. And each one has different rules and requirements.

Some countries might require that you apply within a specific window in advance of your departure; others demand proof of a particular vaccination. A few countries request you apply from your homeland; others increase the fee if you apply from the road. Several places issue visas upon arrival, while plenty offer them online. And then there are those that will deny you entry if they see you've traveled to a region they deem unfriendly. Don't expect anything to be straightforward.

On top of the rules for entering countries, there are also rules for how long you can stay. This matters if you want to come and go, or stay longer than the typical tourist period. The European Union, for example, only permits ninety days of travel within every 180 days. So, a plan to spend three months traveling around central Europe, followed by a month traveling through Russia and Belarus, before heading back southern Europe, wouldn't work. You would have to devise a route that keeps you another two months outside the EU before returning.

If you aren't a detail-oriented planner by nature, then maybe that single-issue visa to one country sounds more appealing now. But if you want to minimize the need to plan and maximize your spontaneity while still going 'round the world, then limit yourself to countries that don't require a visa.

Three Basic Visa Tips for 'Round-the-World Travelers

1. Inform yourself of visa requirements and paperwork involved for *all* the countries you want to visit. Stay apprised of current laws and travel advisories.
2. Plan a logical route—one that won't force you to turn around because you recently visited a country deemed unacceptable. Rather, if you plan to travel to adversarial countries, do it in the correct order.
3. Plan your route within the valid dates of the visas you do obtain. An itinerary off by one day can cause you or your bank account a major headache.

HEALTH CARE, WELLNESS, AND PETS, TOO

Chances are, any long-term visa you apply for will require you to hold adequate health-care coverage. This could be the case whether or not a country touts a free national health care system for its citizens. 'Round-the-world travelers won't want to deny themselves coverage, either. Even if you're young, healthy, and rarely catch a cold, a basic insurance plan to cover the unlikely what-ifs is a smart peace-of-mind move.

If you expect your medical needs will be minimal, search for a lower-cost, high-deductible plan for expats. Ditto for 'round-the-world travelers: Find a basic travelers' policy that will last the duration of your adventure and is valid wherever you go. Knock on wood you won't have to use your policy at all. But if the need arises, you're set.

Also keep in mind that, should you get sick, it may be much easier—and cheaper—to pay for services out of pocket than to navigate your policy's network. Try to put aside any skepticism about foreign or state-sponsored medicine abroad. Stories abound that affirm how inexpensive yet effective it usually is.

Finding the Best Insurance Policies

Sure, the Internet is a good start (search terms: expat + health + insurance). But given how fast the world of health insurance is changing, your best bet is to go to other expats. What companies and policies are they happy with? I guarantee the topic has come up on one of the expat forums or Facebook groups you're following. Another good source is your current insurance agent, who may be affiliated with a company that offers expat policies.

If your lifestyle involves any physical activity deemed "extreme" by insurance companies, make sure you get a special rider. A typical policy might consider bungee jumping, camel riding, or even skiing too extreme to cover. Read the fine print and ask the right questions if anyone in your family falls under such an uber-athletic category.

And take note: If you return home at any point during your year abroad (either planned or unexpectedly), your expat policy might not cover you once you step foot in your homeland. If it doesn't, you'll need to purchase an inexpensive travelers' policy for the duration of your visit home.

Vaccinations

Mandatory vaccinations (if any) should be listed as a visa requirement, depending on where you're headed. School-mandated vaccines are a murky territory. Cover your bases by bringing your kids' vaccination records.

If you plan to travel to any exotic locations while you're away, certain shots may be suggested or even required. Research current traveler advisories on the topic and adjust your to-do list and budget accordingly. Note how long a particular required vaccine takes to go into effect—and how long it stays effective. It could mean getting vaccinated when you're abroad.

Medicine and Supplements

Consider stocking up on medicines or supplements you take on a regular basis. Though plenty of common remedies can be purchased over the counter—and often cost far less—they may go by a different name or be unavailable in your target country. And you might prefer to avoid the rigmarole of a doctor visit while overseas just to get a prescription.

Don't count on being able to order meds online—or to have them shipped from another country. The same goes for nonprescription stuff. This includes anything that might be useful when traveling to a place where food and water practices could cause distress, such as traveler's diarrhea. So, do your research. If you anticipate needing a particular Rx, or you have a favorite brand of supplement or remedy, devise a way to bring a supply.

Check with a health practitioner whether having certain antibiotics or herbs on hand is advisable. If you can't bring all your provisions in advance, it might mean that visitors from back home will courier them in their suitcases. But consider this your notice to…

Anticipate Special Needs

If you or someone in your family has a condition requiring ongoing attention or prescriptions, make sure you'll have access to a competent provider. And verify that any needed drugs are available in your target country, or as you travel. Learn from our story.

One of my daughters has a condition that requires periodic monitoring and ongoing treatment with prescription medications. We did due diligence and found one of the few doctors in Italy familiar with her malady, and she was wonderful. However, we didn't anticipate that getting one of the drugs in question would be near impossible. And, to make matters worse, we discovered Italy strictly prohibits most medicines from being shipped across its borders.

After scouring options in nearby countries, we found a less satisfactory substitute drug through the Vatican pharmacy. (Fun fact: The Vatican is a separate sovereign nation with the Pope as its leader.) We eventually managed a workaround through a family contact at a US military base in Italy. But in short, it was a mini-nightmare.

I don't know whether a simpler solution would have been possible, since Italy wasn't going to change its laws for little ol' us. But had we known in advance, we could have avoided the stress of scrambling by either adjusting our expectations or somehow figuring out a way to get a year's supply of pills ahead of time.

Pets

Many of us have pets we treat as family members, and we can't imagine being apart from them for a year. If your family falls under this category, add this research piece to your list (search terms: bringing + pets + abroad). Countries around the world require quarantine periods, some as lengthy as six months, before your beloved pet can live with you. And depending on where you'll be living, your homeland may require a quarantine period upon your return.

The price of such quarantines aside, consider the cost to your beloved animal. When you factor in the stress of airplane travel and the change to a new environment, the upheaval might end up being too much for your pet. Once you gather the details on transporting particular animals to your destination, you should have enough data to make a well-reasoned, if emotional, decision.

TRANSPORTATION WHILE ABROAD

The easy part is getting there—whether *there* is your starting point for the year or your home for the year. But once you land, how will you get around? Can you imagine living without a car? Do you picture using a bike? The bus? Or mostly your feet?

When traveling for brief periods, it's no trouble to wing it with a mix of car rental, cabs, public transportation, and walking. But parking yourself in a new location for a year means giving some serious thought to how you'll navigate your daily routine.

Buying a Car

The notion that you'll purchase a vehicle upon arrival and sell it before you return home might seem rational and simple enough. But it might not be that straightforward. Depending on where you're headed, buying, registering, and insuring a vehicle as a tourist may not be legal, much less easy. As a *resident* in a foreign country, it could go without a hitch. But depending on your type of visa, you might not be considered a resident in the legal sense. And if you *are* deemed a resident, purchasing said vehicle could have thorny tax implications when it comes time to sell the car.

Perhaps you plan to keep the car and bring it back as a large souvenir. Some overseas automakers have specific programs for transoceanic sales (e.g., Volvo, BMW) that could fit your needs. But bringing back other vehicles—new, used, or collectible—could trigger a major headache. Hefty shipping costs aside, strict EPA rules govern which vehicles can be brought back to the US, and yours might not make the cut without drastic engine alteration.

If your target destination calls for a car, spend a couple of hours researching your best options rather than make assumptions. Other expats in your target destination can alert you to potential problems, and may even guide you toward a good deal on a vehicle. But set your expectations that strolling into an auto dealership, or buying a used vehicle from a stranger, will be anything but a breeze.

Renting a Car

If your year abroad brings you to a metropolitan area, it might be preferable to arrange your life so you don't need a car at your daily disposal. Some combination of public transportation, walking, and cycling could be just the ticket. And renting here and there for longer distances or day trips would complete the picture.

We managed in Genoa with such a hodgepodge transportation plan. And besides the minor hassle of picking up and dropping off the car at the airport, there was little downside. To be honest, the walking lifestyle is one of the things we miss most. It kept us fit and intimately connected with our adopted city. Plus, we didn't have to deal with crowded city parking, not to mention the expense of maintaining a vehicle.

Once you get settled, you too might find that having access to an occasional car will offer a huge step up in freedom. Not being beholden to train or bus schedules and the ease of throwing your luggage in the trunk and pulling up to a beautiful spot off the beaten path are huge advantages. For such short-term rentals, compare your credit cards to see if one offers better insurance coverage for the country in which you'll be renting.

Consider long-term rentals, too, as deals can be had. For example, there is a nifty aspect of French law that allows the purchase and resale of a new vehicle to non-EU citizens only. Dramatically cheaper than typical car rentals, this is a great choice for tourists ranging from a few weeks to several months (search terms: long + term + car + rental + [region abroad]).

International Driving Permit

If you hold a valid driver's license, getting an International Driving Permit (IDP) is a must. Even if you don't plan on driving while overseas, there's no predicting when you could need a car. And during the final stages of packing for your adventure, this one is easy to forget. While you might not be asked for your IDP upon rental, you won't want the buzzkill of being refused a rental contract because you don't have a valid permit.

Acquiring the IDP is straightforward. It doesn't involve a test, and the fee is nominal. Check current rules (travel.state.gov is a good place to start), but as of this writing you can obtain a permit through the AAA or AATA in person or through the mail. Research lead times and requirements, however. An IDP is valid for one year from date of issuance (which can be postdated), and you'll want to time it accordingly.

STAYING CALM—AND ORGANIZED

We've gone through the major hurdles you'll need to clear, such as procuring a visa and arranging housing. And we've delved into the strategies for finding the go-to people and resources for valuable information. So by now you should have a solid sense for what your unique needs are in order to reach that year abroad mountain peak.

As you climb up while gathering your research and building ambassador contacts, your to-do list grows. And similar to the way gravity works, it becomes heavier. So beware the shortness of breath that accompanies the overwhelm! Your saving grace during this part of the process is to stay organized.

Even for go-with-the-flow types used to winging it, there's no way around maintaining a to-do list, which will contain two major categories: closing up shop at home, and preparing for your arrival abroad.

Keeping an up-to-date list will help you stay focused, productive, and able to anticipate any roadblocks. The funny thing about to-do lists, though, is that the tasks have a way of multiplying like rabbits as soon as you write them down. But breaking the big tasks into baby steps can be useful. It can help you keep a handle on things—even though your list may grow to an unwieldy size before you savor the satisfaction of seeing it shrink.

Another thing that helps: other people. If you're adventuring with an involved partner, maintain a joint to-do list and keep each other on task. And as you check items off the list, don't be afraid to ask for help outside your family circle.

As a practical reminder, once you have your financial ducks in a row, whether that includes savings put aside or income-earning lined up, a comfortable time frame for tackling every item on the checklist is about eight months to a year. But some folks accomplish it in far less time. Heck, I connected with one couple who managed to clear out their house and leave within thirty days. With the right friends and resources, you can achieve almost anything!

Organize with Technology

While many of us appreciate the tangibility of pen and paper, the use of technology can't be emphasized enough—especially when it comes to list making and calendar keeping.

Making Lists

Online organizing tools abound. We searched for one that would be ridiculously simple and ended up using WorkFlowy. In effect, it's a shareable online notebook that lets you create endless checklists in outline form, adding subsets and steps to your heart's content. (Also check out Trello, Toodledo, Wunderlist, among others.) Since planning the year abroad is a giant project to be managed on multiple fronts, seek out a project management tool that works for *you* and that you'll actually use.

If you can't tear yourself away from pen and paper, then, whatever you do, *make digital backup copies as you progress.* You won't want to lose track of where you are on the list at any given point—or worse, lose the list itself.

Managing Your Calendar

As you approach the final months before your departure, it will feel like you're in a funnel, trying to squeeze in too many things through too small of an opening. You'll be fitting in those last appointments to the optometrist, dentist, etc., and trying to meet other deadlines before panic creeps in. The key to maintaining daily life with a sense of remote calm is to keep a clear, shareable if applicable, and easy-to-manage calendar (e.g., Google Calendar, Cozi, etc.).

Online Community

Another reason to embrace technology is to maintain a tight and active hold to your online community of ambassadors and fellow adventurers. Not only might you be a source of encouragement for each other, but connecting with someone who gets it can offer relief from the stress. In addition, you can get the heads-up about hard-to-find items and expected challenges in your target country. Better to avert a headache abroad with an easy solution before you leave home.

MAKE THE LEAP ... FINALLY!

When you see the light at the end of the tunnel, it means the countdown to that leap across the ocean has begun in earnest. At this point, you might start to hyperventilate when you look at what remains on your to-do list. Heck, if I look over the to-do list from our big adventure year (see a pared-down version in the Appendix), I start to hyperventilate all over again!

For the final stretch of your preparations, before you manage escape velocity, I offer the major takeaways from our experience. Hindsight, as they say, is 20/20.

On Packing: What to Bring... or Not to Bring

- Less is more. Full stop. Unless you are going to a far-flung place inaccessible to modern conveniences, plan to bring only the absolute basics. It's easy to slip into the temporary vacation mindset, packing every possible thing you might use. Break this temptation! Figure you can buy it if you need it. In addition to being a great opportunity to practice nonattachment, stripping down to the bare essentials is quite liberating.

And don't expect that shipping stuff will relieve you of any hassle. While it seems like a reasonable solution (and it might be for certain things), it gets outrageously expensive. And that assumes everything makes it through customs.

If I had a do-over, I would limit us to one large suitcase each, with kids offering up some space to parents. But that may not be feasible if you have to bring necessities, such as medicine or supplements not easily acquired at your destination. Have the mindset that you'll rent, purchase, or borrow heavier things like bulky winter clothing, ski boots, bed linens, etc.

- Bring a few printed photos of friends and family, and/or small sentimental tchotchkes. You'll want to pepper your home abroad with a few things that will warm you up with a touch of continuity to your current life. In a subtle way, it helps to bridge your experience, keeping you grounded on those days where you feel like a lonely fish out of water.
- While you should also digitize important papers, prepare a "Must Not Lose!" folder that includes passports, crucial contact info (for banks, credit cards, etc.), and any other difficult-to-replace documents. Always bring this folder with carry-ons—never in checked luggage.

On Closing Up Shop

- As impossible as it might seem, try your darndest to pad your schedule with extra margin, especially as all those to-dos pile up. This helps accomplish three things:

1. You'll be able to find needed time for the unexpected tasks that arise.
2. You'll be in a better position to see good friends for a last-minute coffee, instead of at a frenzied goodbye gathering.
3. It will keep you from going completely bonkers.

- Have a going-away party of sorts, but let someone else plan it! Assuming you'll return to your same community after the year abroad, it's important to nurture your friendships and other relationships, which will be a challenge when you're building a life overseas in another time zone. And though you may have a million other priorities during those final weeks, friends will want to see you off. Grant them at least that.

Some Final Words on That Last Step Before You Jump

When you reach the last couple of tasks on your checklist (one of them being getting yourself to the airport), you can breathe a heavy sigh of relief. Like the first stage of the rocket falling off, you'll have released a huge weight off your shoulders.

The long airplane ride to your destination might be your last chance to chill for a long time, so enjoy the blue skies and in-flight movies from your airplane seats. Because once you land, your senses will undergo a radical awakening.

eelee

SAVE IT FOR SOMEDAY TIPS

If you are in the thick of planning your year abroad, you can't save anything for someday. But if your year abroad is slated for the future, some things you can do today will make climbing the mountain easier when the time comes:

Finances

- As you put aside money for savings, retirement, and a college fund for your children, plan to demarcate a percentage of these to go toward a year abroad. Your adventure can fall under the category of education or career growth. You might even consider it a displaced year of retirement. Shift your thinking if you need motivation to make the finance part happen. With intention and a bit of sacrifice, you'll be surprised at how much it's possible to save in a few years.
- Think about skills you might develop so you're able to work remotely if need be. Whether you plan to shape-shift your job or find a different type of online work while you're overseas, you'll want to be confident in your computer skills.
- Explore ways to build an additional income stream. Don't assume the traditional one-job career is the only way. If others are able to manage a second or third income stream, why not you? Read or follow Chris Guillebeau's *Side Hustle* (book and podcast) for ideas and inspiration.

Housing

- Experiment with the cost-effective mode of traveling known as *home exchange*. Not only does this get you comfortable letting another family live in your house someday, it might connect you to folks in your someday target country.

- Gradually cull excess stuff in your home and limit the further acquisition of unnecessary items. This will spare you a bigger headache down the road when you prepare your house for renters.

- If you have a sense for how far in the future your adventure will be, make big purchases accordingly. If you hold on to your old computer, car, or couch for just another year or two, then you can spend your money on a *better, newer* model when you return from the year abroad. (And you won't care so much about wear and tear from renters.)

Education (Language)

- If you have an inkling of where you want to spend your someday year abroad, start learning the language now. Getting an upper hand, even years in advance, will not only relieve the burden later but will facilitate in making your year happen. By becoming literate, learning about your target country, and meeting potential ambassadors, you'll be doing yourself a big favor.

- Start your kids early with a foreign language—even if it's not the language you'll be using abroad. Studies indicate that the earlier a child's brain becomes wired for another language, the easier it'll be to learn *any* foreign language when they're older.

Visas

- Look at the requirements for your likely visa application to see if there's anything you can prepare for in advance (for example, a program that allows for a student visa).
- If the visa you'll likely apply for requires a regular inflow of funds outside of salary, consider rearranging your finances now. Perhaps you shift your portfolio to include dividend-producing stocks, which then spin off regular deposits into your main banking account. Setting up some kind of auto deposit, even if small, can't hurt and will probably help when someday comes.

Transportation

- Learn how to drive a stick shift. It increases your cool factor and gives you more options—and less expensive ones, too—when driving abroad.
- Heed yet another reminder to explore travel hacking. At a minimum, accrue frequent flyer points through your credit card. Resources such as extrapackofpeanuts.com, onemileatatime.com, frugaltravelguy.com, or travelhacking.org can guide you on getting a leg up for free or upgraded travel, which is always a bonus.

Organization

- Get accustomed to using an organization tool, such as Trello, WorkFlowy, or another app/program that involves tracking lists. And if you aren't managing a calendar yet, start now. This will make it much easier to fold in all those necessary tasks when you're ready to get set and go!

CHAPTER SIX

BE NIMBLE, JACK

Now that you understand all the practical tasks involved in achieving the year abroad, you should have some clarity on what your personal list might look like. After all, this is *your* unique adventure, a dance only you can perform. And you will improvise the choreography as you gather data, talk to your ambassadors, explore options, and face limitations.

The biggest skill to hone for this adventure is agility. You must learn to be nimble—to adjust your thinking, or your plans, at any point. The less ruffled you are while making these shifts, the better.

In many ways, moving forward with your dream of taking a year abroad is a huge risk to your identity. You're putting yourself out there with a clear, determined goal. High expectations form—not only for yourself and your family, but also by others.

In our case, in the year leading up to our departure, countless hours of research led me to dozens of interactions on the phone and online that finally put me in touch with a few schools where I could picture our kids, maybe. So we focused hard on our mountain of details:

- I mustered the energy and resources for a ten-day reconnaissance trip to visit schools.
- My husband, an executive coach and corporate team-builder, had prepped his clients for minimal contact. His career suspension was a delicate two-step that needed to convey the hope of a long-distance relationship: "I'm still yours, even though I can't fully be there for you. Keep the faith—I'll come back."
- We culled the crap out of our house and searched high and low for tenants before the Czech family miraculously appeared.
- We held our breath as we negotiated with the girls' school to hold spots for them after we got back.
- Based off a few photos, we made an agreement with a total stranger to rent our first apartment in Genoa.
- We allayed our kids' fears as we built their excitement: "It might be a little scary at first, but it's gonna be fun! We'll have lots of gelato!"

This dance slowly crescendoed as our dining room table accumulated the voluminous pages required for the visa application, which offered no guarantee of approval. But what if the vision we held didn't transpire the way we were laying it out?

PLAN B?

To be nimble in the big-picture sense means having some kind of plan B. As you prepare to dance across the border while juggling all those task balls in the air, you can expect a few to drop. And dropping a ball here and there might throw you off until you regain your balance. But what happens if you trip and bring *all* the balls down with you? What is your plan B if your plan A falls apart?

Remember Linda, who planned to move with her family to Malta for a year? Their house was rented, their furnishings in storage. They were *already settled* in their destination country when they discovered their adventure as planned could not continue. *Inconvenient* doesn't even begin to describe their situation.

Tanya and Stephen also had to shift their plans on a dime. For years they had dreamed of a sabbatical in Denmark with their daughters. They had saved money, had done reconnaissance trips, and could imagine their nine-month stay in all its glory—but they couldn't get a visa. It didn't matter who they knew or what inside connections their friends had. Those steadfast Danish would not budge.

And then there's Carl and his family, who we stumbled upon during our year in Genoa. Like us, they had plotted for years to bring their kids to Italy. Their plan went smoothly until they arrived to complete the process of getting the *permesso di soggiorno*. Because Carl, a professor, had decided to turn his year abroad into a classic academic sabbatical by doing some research with the university in Genoa, he had mistakenly applied for the wrong visa. This technicality meant reapplying for his visa from his native Canada *after* his whole family was already situated in Italy. Imagine his throbbing headache.

We ourselves had a last-minute panic when a consulate officer told us the visa we were applying for was only for retirees. Gulp. We scrambled to reword some things only to learn she had misspoken. But what if this glitch had turned into a major snag? What would we have done? And here's my confession: We didn't have a plan B—which is exactly why I'm suggesting you create one.

I suppose we would have slopped together some kind of travel year, since our house was already rented and we were in the midst of goodbyes. Or maybe in haste we would have researched other countries that might have given us a visa (we *did* have all the paperwork ready!). But since a plan B was nowhere on the horizon, the disappointment would have been *crushing*. If at least a ghost of a backup scheme had existed, it would have come into focus instead of our plans dissipating into disappointment.

But enough of all this hypothetical talk. What happened to the real-life families who faced such a dilemma?

Linda and brood meandered home to the States. They stopped in Genoa, where we showed them a few sights and took them for pizza. They were deflated, the wind out of their sails. But they were determined to squeeze the fun out of their unexpected journey back to Colorado.

With their house rented in their hometown, they opted to make a big change by moving to an entirely different community. And for now they've put the year abroad idea on hold. Instead, they target summers to explore different countries. The simplicity is irresistible: no visa applications, no school transfers, no yearlong leases. Plus, their mini immersions in different cultures might lead them to a place that resonates, should they decide to go abroad for a longer stint when their kids are older.

Stephen and Tanya ended up switching not only countries but continents! They had previously visited a relative in Chile, and the lightbulb went off. They would have a Spanish-language-immersed, South American experience instead. The process to extend a three-month tourist stay to six months in Chile was pretty straightforward, so that's what they did. They enrolled the girls in a parochial school in Santiago and settled in for their unplanned adventure. Instead of being shaped by Danish memories near the North Sea, Stephen and Tanya's family now looks back to a sunny sabbatical that faced the South Pacific.

And our fellow Italian expats? Carl had to fly solo all the way back to Canada's west coast to change his paperwork and apply for the correct visa! Despite the unwelcome and unexpected expense, it was the right choice for Carl's family, rather than unraveling all the dreams they had made for their year.

Prepare for the Unexpected

Can we learn anything from these detours? Could any amount of research have avoided the headaches? Who knows? At some point, things unfold how they do, and we chalk it up to "these things happen." Even when everything goes as planned and life abroad is humming along, the rare unforeseen event might force a sharp detour, like it did for the Hudson family.

In the spring of 2009, Dave and Katy Hudson embarked on a three-month sabbatical in sunny Mexico. They pulled their daughters out of school, enrolled in Spanish classes, and settled into a house rental in Guanajuato. The family adjusted easily into the daily rhythm of their peaceful village, until…the swine flu broke out. The headlines didn't hold back:

"Deadly new flu strain erupts in Mexico"

"Swine flu could kill millions"

"U.S. declares public health emergency…"

Visitors left Mexico in droves, the language school shut down, and the town became eerily quiet with everyone wearing masks. The Hudsons escaped to California, where they wrestled with next steps. After a couple of weeks of uncertainty, things calmed down and they returned to finish out their Mexican sabbatical. It's easy in retrospect to conclude that the swine flu panic was overblown. But when you're in a foreign land, the desire to transport yourself to a comfort zone when an unknown horror is on the loose is a natural response.

We all know unfortunate things like Ebola and terrorist attacks lurk in the underbelly of early-twenty-first-century life. And no doubt these types of events are what concerned friends and family cite when they urge you not to embark on a crazy undertaking like a year abroad. But a reasoned mind knows that unexpected calamities can happen anywhere, including in your own backyard.

Your job is to take your tolerance for the unknown into account and plan anyway.

Let these real-life stories serve as a reminder to give yourself an emotional and psychological check-in about your year abroad plans. Ask yourself: What if this adventure doesn't transpire like we hope it will?

If you're still in the planning stages when things veer too far off track, you'll want a plan B, however loose. Even if plan B is to revert to stay put, at least you won't lose as much sleep over the shift.

And if the unexpected happens when you're on the road, consider what plenty of travelers say after the fact: The unpredictable events are often the richest part of the journey. When you reflect on the big picture, the unexpected incidents, however unpleasant at the time, often provide the best learning experiences of your life (if not the best stories!). Whatever lemonade you'll make out of lemons, it will taste sweeter in retrospect.

BE NIMBLE AS YOU TRAVEL

Up till now we've talked of the need to be nimble in terms of your big-picture plans. The ability to move on to plan B if necessary and/or embrace the unexpected will serve you well. In a similar vein, the ability to pivot during your everyday travels determines how happy of a camper you'll be.

Whether you intend to meander the globe or to use your target location as a home base for regional trips, nimbleness is key. Whatever the scenario, you'll sit somewhere on the spectrum between two predominant attitudes held about travel.

One camp, the Meticulous Planners, value heavy research and mapping out the details of their voyage. The other camp, the Improvisers, relish the spontaneity of discovery and rely on instinct more than booking ahead. A high school debate team could build a strong case for either side, but I'm here to tell you that you must wear both hats *and* be smart about when to switch them.

The Case for Planning Ahead

As the basic structure of your adventure becomes clear, chances are the list of must-see places starts to form. For example,

- If you're heading to Southeast Asia, how do you *not* see Angkor Wat?
- Will you spend an entire year in South America and skip the Galápagos?
- Perhaps your grandmother always talked of a tiny ancestral village in Scotland. Should you maneuver to go there even if you'll be living in sunny Spain?
- And for those doing a 'round-the-world year, several not-to-be-missed destinations are begging you to play connect the dots as you map out your route.

If you leave any of these visits to chance (or to the last minute), you risk missing out or possibly spending a small fortune to make them happen. The key in these situations is to plan ahead.

And any place you want to visit that falls under the category of popular tourist destination also builds the case for planning ahead. It's a rather simple equation:

Popular tourist spots (crowds + competition for quality lodging, guides, food) = high prices

The sum of all these factors equals frustration. So if expense or quality options matter to you, be ready to wear the planner hat.

A plan-ahead attitude doesn't mean you'll be locked into a particular agenda. It just means a bit of advanced preparation is needed. For example, in the case of popular tourist spots, once you target potential dates for these destinations, make reservations. But make ones that are *cancelable*.

For those off-the-beaten-path destinations, such as an ancestral village, it behooves you to make contact ahead of time. Imagine the utter disappointment if you showed up only to discover an empty town because everyone has fled to the coast for summer, or that the librarian who knows all about your family's history is not available.

The other aspect of the plan-ahead attitude is strategy with *timing*. Whether you'll follow a seasonal calendar (e.g., for school holidays) or need to coordinate with others' schedules (e.g., visitors from home), take advantage of knowing probable dates. This lets you score the choice options at the lowest prices.

Plan-ahead mode also encompasses being attentive to visa rules and travel advisories. Take John Kin and Frances Durcan, who spent a year in Guatemala with their two children. The parameters of their visa required them to leave the country after six months before they could return for the latter six months of their stay. For them, it was a no-brainer to use that time as a vacation. And just being aware of that rule gave them a nice lead time to tour with intention.

Or maybe you'll have to exit a region for an extended period, as was the case for Tracey Carisch. She realized too late that Americans were limited to ninety days in the EU, thanks to that pesky Schengen Agreement. Her family would not be allowed to spend five continuous months jaunting around Europe as part of their eighteen-month trip. Some eleventh-hour shuffling meant the Carisches spent additional dates in Croatia and Ireland, countries not part of the territory—but they sacrificed Portugal and Spain in the process. Hardly a tragedy, but tuck it away as a reminder that such stress is avoidable.

Requisite traveler visas or vaccines, if overlooked, could ruin any trip if you don't plan ahead. And for vaccines, remember some take weeks to become effective, and then may only last for a short duration. So no matter where you hope to visit, a little advance planning goes a long way in saving you sizable headaches and a good chunk of cash.

In Defense of Spontaneity

The downside of vacation planning is that it can be time-consuming and draining. When you're soaking up your year abroad experience, who wants to spend precious hours arranging where you'll be sleeping for a few nights down the road?

It was springtime in Genoa, and I could hear the bustling noises of life outside our window filling the walk-streets below. I wanted to go down and soak it up, knowing our days there were numbered. But I was chained to my laptop because we had no plan for our monthlong summertime trek through central Europe. If I didn't book tickets, we wouldn't be able to visit our friends in Norway. If I failed to find a hotel with parking in Amsterdam, the girls would miss out on the Anne Frank House. And if we didn't figure out our rental car, we would get royally screwed with last-minute price hikes.

Couldn't I just go with the flow and up the thrills by winging it? It's valid to tout the economic virtues of planning ahead. But sometimes last-minute deals are the best to be had. While I personally didn't have the stamina for that on our exit trip, such improvisation skills are worth adopting during the year abroad. It tests your agility to pull your kids out of school on the fly and suspend your routine. And impromptu get-up-and-go trips can make for the most vivid, memorable holiday adventures.

After the many moons you've spent to organize this fabulous year for you and your family, why wouldn't you be open to spontaneity? Otherwise, aren't you just re-creating a predictable life in another country?

If you hope to plan ahead wisely, yet experience the joy of spontaneity, then the question is: How can one plan to be spontaneous?

As with most things, the key to setting yourself up for successful spontaneity involves a balancing act.

Practical Tips for Striking the Balance

- If possible, **obtain a rail or bus pass that offers more affordable transportation**, with minimal advance booking requirements.

- **Subscribe by email to regional railways, airlines, or car rental companies**. Though it increases your spam (until you unsubscribe), get in the habit of glancing at their current and last-minute specials. For example, we often saw nineteen-euro flights to intriguing destinations. If you're willing to travel at less popular times, you can get more bang for your buck.
- **Join frequent traveler programs** for any regional airline, car, railway, or chain hotel companies you'd consider patronizing. At a minimum, you could accrue transferrable points for future use in partner programs. But you're also likely to receive perks such as early boarding, free carry-on luggage, or advance notice of specials. When companies today are nickel and diming customers, these perks have value.
- **Explore hiring a private guide** at popular tourist destinations rich in history. Often, a spontaneous trip results in limited time at a single location, and having a guide maximizes those hours brilliantly. While quality tour guides don't come cheap, they're worth every penny when they help you understand the sights you're seeing. And without that deeper understanding, you're just taking in mere eye candy. Bonus: Often a guide's license permits them to jump the line, saving precious time and allowing you to squeeze in more sights.
- If a private guide is too much of a splurge, **seek out a well-reviewed guided group tour**. Popular destinations typically offer guided tours at a lower cost, again letting you pack the highlights into a concentrated time period. And in either the private or group scenario, having access to a local guide means you get to pick their brains for insider advice on the

best restaurants, shops, etc.

- **Try to leave space in your calendar.** This might be a challenge if your schedule is filled with invitations or visitors. While that speaks to a socially active sabbatical, try to be clear about your travel intentions if travel is a priority for you. Consider inviting friends to join you in your excursions. And be picky about who and what will obligate you to stay close to your home turf. Does your son really need to attend another schoolmate's birthday party instead of finally escaping to Kyoto for the long weekend?

- Aside from more involved long-distance vacations, **consider smaller, easier trips** near your home abroad. Keep a growing list of places recommended by locals. While not as glamorous as popular tourist destinations, those short, sweet visits to spots whose greatest claim to fame is "Napoleon slept here" might be just the ticket for building fun memories on the spur of the moment.

- **Keep a standard checklist** that makes it easy to pack in a pinch and escape without worry. Besides having a packing list that gets you through security lines without hassle, be sure you know the process for closing down your flat. And remember to notify your credit and bank cards if you are traveling outside your current country.

MAXIMIZE FUN AND MINIMIZE CHAOS WHEN TRAVELING WITH KIDS, OR KIDS AT HEART

While the above tips preach to efficiency when traveling, having kids (or distractible adults who don't like to sit still) in tow can unravel any and all efficiency. My friend Lora Gordon—who has visited twenty-plus countries (from the pyramids in Egypt to the Amazonian jungles of Ecuador) over the course of fourteen years with her husband and two daughters—helped to create the following:

- **Involve your children in the planning.** They become more invested while also developing research skills. Plenty of books and guides to popular tourist destinations exist for young readers. If you do most of your fact-finding online, add "+kids" to any travel keywords, which reveals kid-friendly options and tips for your destination. Often these unconventional, unexpected suggestions are fun for adults too. At a minimum, intersperse adult sightseeing with fun kid activities. A child will tolerate another "boring" museum if she knows the beach awaits the next day.

- **Set your daily expectations** about all the marvelous things you'll see and do at your travel destination. Be realistic about how many hours your children are able to focus, and how much energy they can muster to move from place to place. Fold in extra food, drink, and bathroom stops. And don't underestimate the rejuvenating power of retreating to the hotel for an hour to nap or just veg out in front of foreign TV. Organize one or two big things for the day. Then dangle the carrot of various treats or fun activity breaks, such as blowing giant rope bubbles with the artist in the park. Any additional sightseeing you squeeze in becomes a bonus.

- **Anticipate some un-fun**. Let your kids know that sometimes traveling plain sucks. Whether it's the delayed train while you sit in a smelly train station, a long bus ride that brings on motion sickness, or a weird, unappealing meal, teach your children the concept of hunkering down. The sooner they learn that complaining doesn't make things better, the quicker they'll learn to manage. To prepare for un-fun, include these in an emergency kit: snacks to fend off hunger and meltdowns, Tylenol/Advil, adhesive bandages, hand sanitizer, gum, wet wipes, sunscreen, lip balm, a good book, and an iPod or similar device. This should dispel most travel crises, at least until you can get to a drugstore. If your children are old enough, put them in charge of their own kits.

- **Balance caution with empathy.** If you visit any high-poverty zones, be prepared for disturbing sights or interactions. Consider that the safest demeanor might be to walk with a confident gait and avoid eye contact with those approaching you for money or food. Exercise your best judgment and expect your empathy to be challenged. Use such encounters as teaching moments with your children. Show them it's normal and healthy to grapple with blatant inequality. Perhaps talk about systemic solutions to poverty. Whether you give cash on the spot or donate as a family to NGOs working in the region, teach your children to make a difference.

- **Build anticipation with literature and film.** Search for fictional stories or documentaries that take place wherever you're headed. Age-appropriate stories are key. One series we loved was *The Magic Treehouse*, which sends its characters on various adventures around the world and across time. *Vacation Under the Volcano* volume brought Pompeii to life for us, despite a miserable downpour the day we visited. Any stories that activate the imagination and build excitement for the trip will add context and depth to your travels.

- **Prepare for some basic cultural interaction.** As a family, learn a bit of the local language for the places you're heading to. Even basic phrases such as hello, goodbye, thank you, and "my name is..." go a long way. Your kids (and you) will get so much friendly attention in return for their modest efforts, which boosts their confidence and creates a sense of belonging. The cherry on top is when your kids connect with local children in their native tongue.

- **Buddy up with technology.** And I'm not talking about dispensing iPads to keep kids calm (though there's no shame in that on occasion). But a data- or Wi-Fi-enabled smartphone can be a lifesaver in finding just the right spot for a treat or a quick respite. Whether you need transportation, a food market, a late-night hotel, or on-the-spot temperature or currency conversion, easy solutions are at your fingertips with an app. Also, if you have two smartphones, parents can divide and conquer—before reconvening with ease.

- **Hunt for treasure.** Embrace technology even further by downloading a geocaching (or similar) app. Such treasure hunts are all over the world and help build the excitement, keeping kids focused and curious. If that's not your thing, do a low-tech treasure hunt. Create a list of iconic or sure-to-encounter sights for your kids to fill in the proverbial bingo card (e.g., the Eiffel Tower, a croissant, etc.). Maybe it's as simple as letting your child find that one special souvenir to bring home.

The underlying goal in all these tips: *Keep 'em moving and motivated!*

Practical tips aside, there's only one fundamental rule to take to heart: Be present. While it's not always possible to find that balance between planning and spontaneity, it *is* always possible to focus on the moment. You might miss out on the *choicest* tourist option because you didn't take the time for thorough research, but staying present and going deep in the moment sets you up for those visceral, unforgettable memories.

BE NIMBLE WITH YOUR THINKING .

Whether you are moving forward with plan A, plan B, or plans to meander the globe, the whole notion of being nimble comes into play every day. Plenty of bumps in the road will test you— both during the planning process and while you are living your much-anticipated adventure. How you navigate those bumps might correlate somewhat with how you're wired, but if you pledge to cultivate these two mental gymnastics moves, I guarantee you'll look back on a successful year abroad:

1. Adjust your expectations.
2. Shift your perception.

In many ways it was nimble thinking that saved us during our year abroad. When we were in Italy, folks back home assumed we were basking in wine-soaked, gelato-laden Mediterranean days of delight. But for the most part, we were sobering up to a stark new reality.

At first, forgoing the ease of the familiar is novel. But it quickly wears on you. When we moved into our first apartment—five stories up a dark stairwell with no elevator—I wondered how we would manage to haul groceries up or acclimate to the up and down several times a day. In a word, it sucked. What else to do but *shift my perception*? There was a smarter way to view this: My rear end would be in better shape than it had been since I was a teenager. My arms would get buff from carrying bags of carb-laden food every day. The downside for our abled bodies? None—other than today's sobering truth that reaching the same fitness level requires hours at a gym.

We faced continual reminders like this throughout our year abroad. All of them taunted us that the dream we envisioned was radically different from its reality. They showed up in everyday annoyances. Some were subtle, some not. But adjusting our expectations and shifting our perception always eased the frustration:

- **Not enough alone time.** Three weeks into our adventure, I wanted to climb out of my skin and run somewhere, *anywhere* I could be alone with my thoughts for an hour. But we were always on the go, sightseeing, getting our bearings, or managing the kids. In retrospect, I should have called a time-out for myself so I could wander alone to a bookstore or a park bench with a view. But I was caught in the barrage of foreign stimuli and not thinking straight.

  The 24/7 family togetherness lasted for two months, and then school started. Knowing it was temporary got me through it, but shifting my perception helped me to cherish it. It helped to bring the ever-so-true cliché "They grow up too fast" to the forefront of my mind, enabling me to appreciate what at times felt like suffocation. Now I recall some of our family's most treasured memories with a profound fondness.

- **Too many chores!** This childish lament resonated with my husband and me as we hand-washed dishes a few times daily and hung laundry out the window to dry, piece by piece. Oh, and not to mention the daily market runs to the butcher, the *focacceria*, or the produce vendor. Is this what we signed up for?

  It turns out, yes. But as soon as we adjusted our expectations to account for daily chores, our perception shifted. We began to view the tedium as a form of meditation. It slowed us down and brought us to the then-present moment. Now those burdensome Italian chores are part of our nostalgia. And some of them we've woven into our current life. (If you hang your clothes, even *indoors,* they last longer *and* it helps the environment!)

- **Forgoing personal preferences**. The annoyances of not being able to satisfy a burrito craving or have *any* ethnic variety in our diet got old fast. Compound that with the daily irritation that we couldn't run errands or do much of anything for the first three hours of the afternoon because of siesta, and such old-world practices made us question an entire culture.

  But changing reality is not an option. And when you can't shift the outside world to suit your preferences, then the only thing to do is shift your perception of the outside world to fit your expectations. Granted, it's often easier said than done. But think about it: If life merely follows your whims, how is that an adventure?

- **Lofty ambitions that remained out of reach.** In the early visions of our living-in-Italy dream, my husband and I pictured lots of time to get creative. We told ourselves we'd learn to cook or paint, or finally write that book. As mentioned earlier, between the kids' truncated school schedule and the added chores, our initial ambitions largely remained in pipe-dream status.

  It took effort to adjust our expectations downward. We learned to accept that snapping a sun-dappled photo on the fly, or even perfecting the art of making stovetop coffee in our moka pot, would have to suffice as acts of creativity. Then we could ease into our life overseas with more simplicity and less disappointment.

ℓℓℓ

Expect the challenges you'll encounter on *your* journey to run the gamut from mild annoyance to tearful frustration. Often the sanest thing to do at such times is adjust your expectations or shift your perception, knowing it's all a part of growth. A shifted mindset isn't always easy to achieve and sometimes requires a very intentional fast-forward to find the silver lining.

When we were searching for our third apartment in Genoa, we lamented that the hunt and the move itself chewed up so much precious time. (Take note: Moving apartments is not advisable for anyone doing a single destination year abroad, but that's how the stars aligned for us.) Since it was unavoidable, I fast-forwarded and found these silver linings:

- We would get familiar with another neighborhood in Genoa.
- We could live within walking distance to a different group of new friends.
- We would experience the city from a whole new perspective.
- Our apartment search would allow us to tour lots of historical palazzos all over the city and meet a wide variety of people.
- And one I didn't anticipate: Since everyone knew we were looking for a new apartment, mere acquaintances became familiar and friendly as they helped us in the hunt.

On occasions when finding the silver lining seemed impossible, as it was when our kids got lice for the third time (ewww), we returned to our Why. While combing through nits, we acknowledged that we could be anywhere (those buggers know no borders). But we signed up to experience life in Italy—and that we did, in all its parasitic glory. Since what one focuses on grows in the mind, we challenged ourselves in this case to concentrate on our limited Italian days, rather than the nasty little creatures at hand.

The irony is that the annoyances and hardships always offer

a gift (if you're willing to shift your perception, that is). While the retrospective rose-colored glasses bring the bittersweet pain of nostalgia at times, choosing when to remember the less rosy events can help you appreciate the present moment. Today, during some of our most challenging times, my husband and I look back and think, "Hey, we could be picking nits, or carrying seven bags of groceries up five flights of stairs, before trudging through a homework assignment in a foreign language!" Life isn't so bad.

෴

SAVE IT FOR SOMEDAY TIPS

- Let the idea of a plan B form along with your dream of a year abroad. If you have a back-up plan that is also appealing, you'll be golden when the time comes.
- Start a bucket list of places you want to see. The more options you have in your constellation of choices, the easier it will be to choose an alternative when you need to be nimble with your travel plans.
- Recognize opportunities when adjusting your expectations or shifting your perception are called for. They happen daily, and learning to master them helps you create a satisfying life, and prepares you for the reality of living abroad.

Part Three: Living the Dream

CHAPTER SEVEN

COME TO YOUR SENSES

You've dreamed. You've plotted and planned. You've deliberated and decided. You've organized and packed. And now you've finally landed.

Think of the Herculean effort you've made to take a year abroad as your entire existence compacted into a little stone inside a slingshot. The practical preparations are akin to pulling back the band before letting go to launch yourself overseas. The subsequent free soaring is exhilarating, but the arrival can be jarring. You want to hit the ground running—but first, you simply hit the ground.

Your five senses won't know what to make of it all. Bridget Kresse recounts her arrival in Lucca as feeling "like all the blood has been drained from your body—yet more alive than ever."

Think about it: For years leading up to this adventure, you've gotten comfortable with your daily routine. For many of us, it feels like 'round-the-clock sleepwalking through repeated tasks or predictable encounters, while retracing turns and traffic lights of familiar routes. Each day ends in front of the mirror as we brush our teeth and wonder, "Wait, wasn't I just doing this the night before? What happened to the last twenty-four hours?"

Chances are, one reason you're seeking this year away is to shake up your routine. Deep down, you intuit that heading off into a world of unknown stimuli will jostle your senses and serve as a springboard for enormous growth. Some might even call it a rebirth.

ALL NEURONS ON DECK

While travel to exotic locations never lacks for sensorial pop, the year abroad is different. When you go on vacation, like the zoo travel I described in Chapter 1, there's a sort of invisible spring connecting you to home. You delight in the flavors and fun of the foreign, and then the minute you return home the all-familiar springs you back to your way of life, diminishing those fleeting impressions. But when you know you'll be gone for a year, that invisible spring becomes more of a lightweight, super-slack bungee cord you forget is there.

Without the usual lifeline to home, you land among the unfamiliar like a baby experiencing her five senses for the first time. Your brain is so busy trying to map out your new reality it's impossible for you to sleepwalk through any of it. Your senses fire on all cylinders, trying to sort out the exotic stimuli of your strange environs. The sights, sounds, and smells that assault you in your first few days become seared in your mind.

I still recall getting off the screeching, lackluster train at Genoa's Principe station in a half-zombie state.

"Wow, finally we're here. This is... *home?*"

Everything was off-the-charts vivid: the relief I felt that Mattea made the trip without vomiting. The sound of wheeled suitcases being dragged across rough pavement. The passengers who scampered every which way to or from their train platform. The colorful magazine stand that enveloped the lonely vendor at the *tabacchi*. Even the cigarette smoke, which we grew to loathe, cast a cloudy sheen over all we took in, making it beautifully surreal.

You'll only go through the newness of your journey once, on those first days after you arrive. This is especially the case if you're doing a single-location year abroad. But unlike a baby, you have adult wisdom that allows you to relish the experience. This freshness is not without its rewards.

Time Slows Down

We're all familiar with how the pace of life moves so slowly when you're young and speeds up the older you get. Remember how, when you were a kid, it seemed to take an eternity for your birthday to arrive? Yet how many of us today stop to calculate our own age because we can't keep track of the years flying by?

David Eagleman, an author and neuroscientist at the Baylor College of Medicine, describes time as "this rubbery thing… It stretches out when you really turn your brain resources on, and when you say, 'Oh, I got this, everything is as expected,' it shrinks up."[11] In essence, the more your brain confronts the unknown, the harder it has to work. And the harder it works, the slower the passage of time seems.

But when things become familiar and expected, your mind skips ahead, and the experience of savoring the present moments disappears. So, for the first few months of your adventure anyway, enjoy the bonus time. Because it feels longer than it actually is!

A Booster Shot for Your Brain

The effort to navigate all the unfamiliar stimuli also boosts your brainpower. It's called *neuroplasticity,* or the brain's ability to adapt itself as needed in strange situations. The more neuroplasticity you have, the better your mind adapts.

Turns out that when you encounter fresh challenges, something unexpected, or other forms of novelty, your brain creates neural pathways. The more pathways it creates, the more neuroplastic it becomes. One study[12] showed that cab drivers who had to learn complex city maps scored higher in general memory tests, for example. Another study[13] that utilized a functional MRI machine showed that subjects' brains lit up when they saw unexpected images—and that such stimuli induced stronger performance (that is, deeper learning) in memory and recall tests.

The upshot for anyone doing a year abroad is that encountering all the unique and unexpected stimuli spells serious brain growth. What better classroom for learning than throwing yourself into a different culture?

A Sixth Sense, Anyone?

The notion that we have a sixth sense or a "Spidey sense" has long been put in the superstitious category. But it's real enough that the US military is studying it,[14] after many reports of soldiers using it to prevent carnage. This sense can work in your favor once you land overseas.

In the days and weeks that followed our arrival in Genoa, it struck me how much a sixth sense jumped in to guide all the other senses that were locked in paralytic overdrive. It was as though a psychic radar knew exactly where and to whom to take my feet in the tangled maze of the unexplored city. We had eerie coincidences of finding the right person at the perfect moment. Once it was the owner of the wine shop who recognized us and directed us to the nearest pharmacy when we were in need. Another day we "accidentally" walked up to the appropriate bus stop with no time to spare when we were lost and running late for our *questura* appointment.

Given that the brain works extra hard to grasp unfamiliar situations, it's no surprise that one would experience a heightened intuition or sixth sense when adjusting to life abroad. Whatever you call it—the twilight zone, synchronicity, or mere coincidence—it's a curious and fascinating experience.

ℓℓℓ

How long should you expect these brain bonuses to last? The shock of the unknown kicks everything into high gear, though this hyperactive sensorial experience diminishes as you ease into a new rhythm. However, each season in your adoptive home brings fresh sights, smells, and tastes. So you're likely to benefit from mini brain boosts throughout the year.

And if you do a 'round-the-world year, the nonstop benefits of experiencing the exotic might reach new limits. Whether you use these little brain bonuses as creativity enhancements, a learning boost, or just as something to marvel at, take note. And enjoy.

Hold On to Common Sense

Coming to your senses would be a meaningless phrase if common sense weren't part of the parcel. When landing at your year abroad location, it's natural to adopt the carefree attitude of vacation mode. And when you take in the foreignness with a childlike wonder, sometimes practical common sense gets shoved aside.

Let this be the gentle reminder to keep those common-sense neurons firing too:

- Make note of emergency contact numbers, or the equivalent of 911.
- Find out whether tap water is safe to drink and street food safe to eat. Prepare for a possible adjustment period as your gut gets accustomed to different microbes. Have necessary medicines or herbs on hand as remedies. (Bonus tip: Oil of oregano is a great natural antimicrobial herb for suspected bugs. Seek

advice from a health professional about what to put in
your arsenal.)

- Heed any warnings from your ambassador contacts
about local scams or dangers.
- Pay attention to any prickly red-flag sensation you
have around a person or situation. While cultural
difference may cloud your reasoning, trust your
instinct. It's there for a reason.

A NEW SENSE OF PLACE, A NEW SENSE OF YOU?

While the initial shock to your senses leaves a lasting impression,
the more meaningful question to ask is: How does the adventure
abroad affect your sense of self over the course of a year and
beyond?

Whether or not personal growth is part of your Why for living
abroad, it is inevitable. Growth in some form happens whether
you stand still for a year or flit around the planet like a butterfly.
Your journey is an inward one too.

The yearlong move outside your comfort zone offers distinct
advantages for reflection and growth, which can help shape who
you aspire to be as you move forward in life.

When you plop yourself down as a foreigner in an unfamiliar
land, blending into the background won't be easy. And whatever
terms you normally use to identify yourself, such as "American,"
"father," "marketing director," etc., will have different contextual
meanings. This forces you to reach deeper and work harder to
make a genuine connection with others.

The result is that the less important labels fade into the background, allowing you to know yourself at a more profound level
when your year is up. It's inevitable that you'll ask yourself bigger
and broader questions.

Who Am I Against the Backdrop of a Foreign Culture?

If you've traveled outside the United States, no doubt you've encountered the stereotypical American tourist. Perhaps you've *been* that stereotypical American. You know, the one in big, bright sneakers and bold-colored clothes, with shiny jewelry and gadgets dangling conspicuously.

Or perhaps you've been the one wanting to crawl under a table when you overhear fellow countrymen talking at stump-speech volume in a charming foreign café, sucking the oxygen out of the room. There's nothing like the threat of being lumped together with a group you *don't* want to identify with to make you ask, How *do* I want to identify?

As soon as you and your family enter a foreign country and open your mouths, locals start to identify you as "the Americans" (or "the Canadians," or whatever your nationality). Your foreign hosts interpret that label based on what they've seen in the media and previous interactions with others of your nationality. Even if you're not a hamburger-eating, gun-toting, rap music fan who drinks Coca-Cola by the gallon, don't be surprised if aspects of a stereotype are projected onto you. Until *you* dispel their myth, that is. And how you do that is up to you.

Will you be defensive about the current president's foreign policy—or apologetic? Will you act more as an ambassador—or an unpatriotic rebel? Will you relish teaching the finer points of your nation's culture—or be more ready to point out its flaws? Maybe all the above and more.

Chances are, you will dispel or confirm the stereotypes without even realizing it, surprising yourself in the process. In our social circle in Genoa, we became the de facto representatives of American culture. That our kids had never eaten a meal at McDonald's was met with disbelief. (But that didn't match the laughable irony that their first Big Mac was at the McDonald's in Genoa's Porto Antico!)

Equally surprising was our display of puritanical uptightness at a birthday party. Our fifth-grade daughter was invited, along with the rest of her class, to a beach party. All the kids—boys and girls—donned their swimsuits to jump into the warm, welcoming sea. And the prepubescent girls, holding on to their carefree childhood, went topless! Our Chiara's one-piece suit made her stand out like an Amish girl in a nightclub.

Life among your foreign hosts offers a unique opportunity to understand, shape, and define how you present yourself in the world. And that doesn't mean you need to adapt your persona to the world's expectations. As much as we intended to follow the "when in Rome" rule, Chiara couldn't turn off her own modesty switch on a dime. Nor should she have to.

Another way to look at this: When you take in all the "differentness" of your adopted culture, you realize that you'll never fully belong. Instead, all the cultural mores or social behaviors you encounter cause you to wonder why they do that. Then you question why *we* do what we do in our home culture. These curiosities will occur throughout your time abroad. And they offer plenty of opportunities to ponder which aspects of your socialization you choose to "own" as a form of personal expression and which you might shed with your fresh awareness.

Ironically, I never embodied my American self more than when I was living in Italy. While an old-world Italian way of life was familiar per my heritage, the stark differences of modern Italian culture stared me in the face whenever I walked out my door in Genoa. Almost every conversation I had revealed different ways of being a mother, a woman, and a wife that either reinforced or made me question my way of being.

For example, it never occurred to me to iron my husband's shirts (much less my own, let's be serious!). Nor was I inspired to take on that task like the Genoese women I met. But another cultural norm *did* inspire me. The way Italians markedly display more affection with their children gave me pause. Americans by contrast are so much more hands-off, afraid of crossing some invisible line. My fresh expat eyes showed me I could grow in a warmer direction.

The backdrop of any foreign community will reveal plenty such differences in your habitual lifestyle, offering the opportunity for reflection. Whether you embrace these reflective moments as a way to help you grow is up to you.

What Matters Most to Me When I'm Free of the Usual Societal Obligations?

As you do the deep, reflective work that stems from the cultural observations you're making, another opportunity for redefinition is at your disposal. Upon your arrival, and with every personal introduction that follows, you decide how to shine in your best light.

Back home, many defining factors allow others to paint an instant picture of who they think you are: your address, your profession, the car you drive, the school your kids attend, the grocery store you frequent, and so on. And people treat you in accordance with their perception of your social standing. But during the year abroad, all bets are off.

Here's your chance to chuck the "sticky" aspects of the old you in favor of definitions *you* choose. No one will care if you belong to a country club or how many garages your house has—and if they do, you're probably meeting the wrong people.

During your time overseas, you get to put your most comfortable foot forward as people get to know you. If your career as an accountant doesn't spark conversational interest, talk about your photography, or sailing, or whatever it is that is more *you*. The curious thing is people then imbue you with different characteristics, which you can adopt or ignore.

A year of trying other ways to define yourself goes a long way in helping you grow. No matter your age, an identity shake-up offers a great opportunity to aid you in becoming more of who you long to be.

How Does Getting Back to the Basics in Relating to Others Help Me Be More Authentic?

Let's go a little deeper and talk about language and choice of words when relating with others. Whether or not you'll be communicating in a language other than English, the rhythms, cadence, and vocabulary at your target location will sound foreign to you. Even if the predominant language *is* English, when you dive into a conversation you won't be swimming with the same school of fish. You're gonna stand out.

And *especially* if the prevailing language in your adoptive country is not your native tongue, selecting phrases and words to get your point across will be a continual challenge. Forget the finesse of subtlety or the ease of knowing that perfect turn of phrase to smooth over any rough statements!

The comparable simpleness of your non-native language skills will frustrate you, but it might be oddly liberating too. It obliges you to get to the heart of what you're trying to communicate. Just as the shortest distance between two points is a straight line, a direct, bare-bones statement of how you react to something, or *what you want* in a situation, is often the most effective and authentic way of relating.

After the school year began, we received several invitations to family dinners—all quite gracious. But there came a point when the language barrier made it all so exhausting. My husband is the extrovert of the family, yet in Italy I was the translator, however rudimentary my skills. We maxed out on social energy pretty fast.

So when Simona asked if we might join her family for dinner one Friday, I wanted to reply, "That's so nice of you to ask. I'm sure it would be fun for the girls to play with the baby and get to know Pietro. But we are planning to head out of town for the weekend and need to do some last-minute shopping before we pack. So it won't work this weekend. Let's try for another time."

But before I could start shaping the semblance of a passable excuse into Italian, my brain gave up. All that came out of my mouth was, "*Grazie Simona, ma non possiamo, mi dispiace. Siamo stanchi.*" Thanks, Simona, but we can't, I'm sorry. We are tired. That's all my exhausted self would squeeze out—and it reflected my tired, introverted self perfectly.

Your foreigner status means people will be forgiving. But it also pushes you to own your opinion and emotions since you can't hide behind niceties or skirt awkward issues with throwaway jokes. Unless you remain in the background, that is. The wallflower route is definitely a choice—and one you'll make often enough to preserve your energy. But if it becomes the predominant choice, it kind of defeats the purpose of your adventurous undertaking, doesn't it?

The more you're compelled to be direct and authentically you, the more you grow in that direction. Of course, there's no need to go on an adventure abroad to discover your more authentic self, but it's certainly a fun way to prompt a growth spurt.

SENSORY PRESERVATION: RECORDING AND SHARING THE MEMORIES IN THE MAKING

With all this talk about newness—new sights, new sounds, new smells, new thrills, a new language, a new you—remember, it doesn't last. So take note—literally! Of course you'll take photos and videos, maybe even post on your favorite social media—but I also recommend taking notes. Deep notes.

The newness is fleeting, and it won't be easy to access those first impressions without some mechanism of preserving them. As with everything else, there's a balance: Capture and document what you can—without letting the act of documenting consume your life.

Among the people I surveyed, a big regret was that they *didn't* make formal observations. Cindy, who lived in Japan for a few years as a young adult, also cautions that the first impressions become normalized pretty quickly and the novelty is lost forever. At a bare minimum, she wishes she had scrawled some notes.

Carole Wells, author of *Chasing Sunsets*, which recounts her sailing trip around the world with her husband and son, offers similar advice to fellow adventurers: Journal daily. And describe your experiences in enough detail so you'll remember them.

I'm one of those people who never thinks to break out a camera or notebook until it's too late. But I'm so grateful my husband has superb documenting skills, which lets me affirm how wonderful it is to have an organized visual record after the fact.

You'll want to bask in the nostalgic glow of the amazing adventure you're creating without shuffling through hundreds of photos trying to remember where you were or what was going on in the picture. Among the numerous ways to document the year abroad experience, here are a few that work well.

A Blog

It seems as though another family travel blog is born every hour. And with good reason too. Blogging offers dual benefits:

1. It helps you store your memories and photos in an organized fashion.
2. It lets you update your friends and family back home.

If you've never blogged, the simplicity is stunning: one entry, a few photos, click, and *voilà*. You have a permanent living record of whatever you publish—or not. (You have the power to delete it whenever you like.) Our blog, giorni-a-genova.blogspot.com, remains a treasure trove that we continue to update on return trips to Italy.

Creating a blog is free and straightforward (search terms: blog + "how to" [option: + family]; limit returns to the last year for current technology). Adjust settings to make your blog public or limit the audience. Your readers may choose to access recent entries by email or by logging in when curiosity strikes. And all you have to do is publish one post at a time, without having to manage myriad email replies from folks back home. If you'd like to interact with those who follow your blog, enable comments.

It's easy to burn out on blogging, though, so pace yourself. Get all family members involved so it doesn't fall on one person's shoulders. And forgive yourself if you take a break from posting. (This epic journey is for *you,* not anyone else, after all.)

One of the biggest motivators to blog, however, is that you'll have a fantastic digital record of your experience, organized by date and however you tag your entries. Bonus: It's a cinch to transform your blog into a memory book, provided you upload sufficiently high resolution photos.

Social Media

If you are already active on social media, you'll be documenting your fabulous journey without shifting your habits. Your posts or tweets serve as your ongoing report of whatever you highlight.

If you aren't so active, or don't have a social media account, there are pros and cons to diving in.

Pros:

- The ability to stay in touch with your friends' lives while simultaneously sharing your own can't be beat.
- You can use a single platform to send private messages as well as public posts that include photos.
- You can add people to your group of followers as you meet them. Any friends you make abroad can simply join your digital clan, eliminating the need to exchange clunky contact information.

Cons:

- If you put effort into keeping up with social media posts, you might on occasion feel as though you've never left home.
- As you add new friends from your target location to your audience, you may feel somewhat restrained at

expressing yourself about your experience in their homeland.

- The format of your chosen platform may be limiting. For example, for a primarily visual person, Instagram might be perfect. But for someone who prefers to write lots of details, it may be cumbersome.

There are also online services that allow you to transform your social media posts into printed books (search terms: social + media + print + memories). So even when you are oriented toward the digital world, procuring a physical memento is possible. Don't underestimate the joy of thumbing through pages and reminiscing.

Journaling

Writing in a journal is not only therapeutic, but it also provides a priceless record of your life story. When you transform your impressions into words, it gives you the gift of time travel back to the freshness of your year abroad whenever you reread them. More intimate than blogging, journaling reflects a deeper you and aids in personal growth. Once you get in the habit, it becomes second nature.

Some best practices:

- Commit to writing every day, even to make a short note of what you did. You don't always have to delve into your thoughts and feelings.
- If you don't have a notebook with you, dictate a memo into your smartphone and email it to yourself.
- If something strikes you when you have no means of recording it, sear a few keywords into your mind until you're able to write them down. Use the mnemonic device of creating a wacky image formed by the keywords to help you remember (it works!).

- Keep your journal in multiple forms. Handwriting in a notebook is great. But if you have a lot to say, type or dictate into your computer.
- Whatever you do, upload your varied entries into an online repository to ensure they don't get lost. Use a scanner app for easy uploading of handwritten notes.

Photos and Videos

Photos are wonderful—but is it possible to have too many? The ease of digital photography can fast become overkill. A friend once posted on Facebook that it would take her almost a year to gaze at every photo on her hard drives for thirty seconds each.

So, in the spirit of less is more, use that camera sparingly! Cull regularly and brutally. And whatever images you decide to keep, be sure to preserve them in the cloud.

And please learn from our devastating mistake: *Make sure your camera works*. We had an entire year of video that came back 65 percent glitched, which pains me to write. So much of the careful documenting that my husband did is lost forever. If only we had taken a moment to play back the video, we could have spared ourselves the heartache and bought a new camera.

Scrapbook Collecting

Scrapbooking is not for everyone, but if appeals to you, prepare for abundant material to work with. All the beautiful little tickets, colorful maps, and well-designed pamphlets of the places you visit are hard even for us non-scrapbookers to throw away.

Breathe fresh life into the bits of ephemera you've tucked away! With the help of an art class, your favorite pieces can shine in collages or paintings.

When you're ready to explore possibilities, search for any variety of ways to process the aftermath of your experience, even if you boast minimal artistic skills (search terms: using + travel + ephemera + scrapbook + crafts). Browse Pinterest for inspiration.

ello

However you document your journey, let it be something you enjoy. And try to make it a habit. You won't regret it.

SUMMING UP YOUR SENSES

This chapter has talked about the initial steps of your adventure abroad—all the way to looking back at it from some point in the distant future. But the crux of this experience/gift you're giving yourself and your family is this: growing into the heart of the present moment.

Living abroad for a year has the power to reawaken you to what life is all about. It's the opposite of wondering how you blinked twenty-four hours away while standing in front of the medicine cabinet brushing your teeth yet again.

Rebecca Ponzi, who is several years into what began in 2012 as a "five-month family sabbatical," summed up the call to shake up your life in a LinkedIn post:

> I gently encourage my friends and colleagues who find themselves in less than satisfying or stagnant situations to not just try their best, but recognize the sleepwalk routine .... that you've been doing the same thing for so long, you can do it with your eyes closed. To get new results, sometimes it takes a rude awakening... I am grateful that I have given our children an experience beyond a textbook or field trip...[15]

True entrepreneurs, Rebecca and her husband, Michel, have built a figurative bridge between the Italian region of Le Marche, where they live in the beachside town of Porto San Giorgio on the Adriatic coast, and their American home base of Dundee, Oregon. The business birthed from their initial year abroad,

Fratelli Ponzi, imports a growing array of their food products made in Italy to local clients in Oregon and beyond. You can get a taste—literally—of the Ponzi family's ongoing adventure at fratelliponzi.com.

eelee

SAVE IT FOR SOMEDAY TIPS

- Start a journal. Even if you're years away from a potential year abroad and only write in it on occasion, start journaling. It will help you track your desires, feelings, and motivations.
- Take pictures. There are tons of ways to learn basic photography skills these days. Whether you take an online course, read a book, or just dive in with your camera, you won't regret developing photography skills.
- Dabble in blogging or social media. If you suspect some form of digital documentation is in your future, get familiar with the process sooner rather than later. Practice by documenting your life leading up to your grand odyssey. And keep in mind that blogging and social media are also potential avenues to finding ambassadors for your someday adventure.

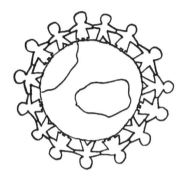

CHAPTER EIGHT

PARTICIPATE IN COMMUNITY

By now, you've gotten the message that uprooting your life is a shock to the system. And that just as the best wines come from grapes cultivated in difficult soil, struggles in the new foreign system can enhance your personal growth.

But let's move on from difficulty and challenge and talk about how to make your life abroad fun. That starts with finding your place and making yourself at home. It means becoming part of the community.

The year abroad is by definition temporary. Whether you stop in a town for a couple of weeks before continuing around the world or you waylay for many months, locals know it's not permanent. Yet also by definition, when you live somewhere—anywhere—you are technically a part of that community for however long you're there. Once you recognize this paradoxical truth, embrace it with intention by folding yourself into the mix.

RELATIONSHIPS: THE BUILDING BLOCKS OF COMMUNITY

The secret to thriving in any society lies in building relationships. Better yet, to maximize fun and good times, aim to go above and beyond by building *friendships*. But when you're focused on getting situated and coming to your senses, this won't happen without proper intention.

To cultivate friendships at any point in life, one follows a common set of guiding principles. These include respecting things such as personal boundaries, as well as social cues and mores. But when you're immersed in a foreign culture for a relatively brief period, special guidelines apply when it comes to making friends.

Bend Your Rules

You've come this far in life in part because you've figured out how you function best. Your rhythms, rules, and habits are dialed for maximum efficiency and ease, even more so when you have children. But "when in Rome," prepare to bend (and break) your rules on a regular basis.

For example, as I mentioned earlier, it surprised us to see young children, gelato cups in hand, running around the piazzas close to midnight on weeknights, albeit in summertime. How would we manage to put our children to bed by nine p.m.—their up-late bedtime hour—with the noise of other kids' laughter and delight floating up through the windows? We wouldn't. Nor would we be able to deny them the steady, punctuated drip of sugary treats woven into the Italian culture without becoming militaristic parents. We could either cling to the rules that had worked for us up till now or we could embrace a more easygoing parental nature.

We chose flexibility. "This is an exceptional year" became our mantra, which allowed for lots of rule bending and wiggle room—when it felt right. And bending our rules provided for a lot more opportunities to meet and connect with people. Once we entered the crowded late-night piazzas with our gelato, it would just be a matter of time before we got to know our new neighbors.

Adapt to a Friendship "Season"

A mere twelve months in a single location offers only a brief stretch to build relationships. Soon after your arrival, a courting period begins when everyone expresses curiosity about the foreigners. Invitations follow (if not, extend them yourself). This is your cue. Say yes to every intriguing thing you have the energy for, unless it seems off in your gut. If you're drawn to know particular people, make your moves during the first few months.

This initial period is when a tribe of friends forms—for you and other family members. Before you know it, the calendar gets populated with activities involving this core group. It becomes more challenging to fold new folks into the tribe as the year advances.

Families with young kids can expect friendships to form in the first several weeks after school begins—for parents and kids alike. The friendship season of courting new companions peaks midyear. And after this point you'll want to maximize time with your tribe before the round of goodbyes begin.

If, however, your year is one of ongoing travel, the friendship season is perennial, if truncated. But even with shorter stays, be open to meeting people.

No matter the circumstances, the friendships you build will have only the depth proportionate to the amount of time and emotion you invest. It all boils down to the connections you make—which could happen while crossing hiking trails in Peru or when sharing a weekly classroom in Prague. Go for it however the opportunities present themselves.

Be Curious

Curiosity of otherness draws the locals to you and vice versa. Take advantage of this inquisitiveness to guide conversation, fill awkward silences, and endear yourself to those around you.

The best way to do this? Keep a mental file cabinet of questions to have at the ready—about your host culture, their language, cuisine, or whatever has you most curious.

You might even conduct an ongoing informal study by asking different people the same questions about a specific interest you have. Throw out questions such as, "Who is your favorite movie star?" or, "What languages do you speak?" and go from there.

Following our swimsuit-challenged birthday party, Marcella and her daughter Eugenia graciously offered Chiara and me a ride home. A near hour in beach traffic meant plenty of time in a car with strangers, no less with stilted language between us. And since Marcella spoke no English, the onus was on me to fill the voids in my awkward Italian.

I had learned that my usual "How long have you lived in Genoa?" was a laughable question, since most people had been there for generations. So instead I asked her if her parents and grandparents had also been born in Genoa, and where had they moved from. I got a window into the patchwork Italian culture and historical migration across the Boot—along with a hefty workout of my Italian. The time passed quickly, and from then on my exchanges with Marcella had a much warmer, more personal tone.

After that, I let my curiosity about genealogy and family history inspire me to collect many a colorful story by the end of our year. Zero in on *your* curiosity and let it guide you toward connection.

Get Into the Expat Groove
Your contact with other expats will vary depending on your location. If you're in a large city or a tourist mecca, you'll have no shortage of compatriots to connect with—assuming you want to, that is. If your goal is cultural immersion, however, hanging out with a bunch of other outsiders keeps you mired in zoo-spectator mode and on the periphery of the local community. A year will go by, and you'll wonder if you missed out.

On the other hand, the desire to befriend someone who can relate to your experience is a powerful pull. I got my fix by joining a Facebook group of English-speaking expats in Italy. It was nice to know I could throw out a question in my native tongue if I needed some insight or advice (or offer the same if someone asked). It was also nice to be able to close the browser and return to my immersion experience.

Keep in mind that everyone's expat scenario is unique. Your adventure ends up being colored by the friendships you develop, whether those friendships are with fellow expats or natives of your host country.

Be Mindful of Attitudes—Especially Those That Surround You

The dispositions and moods of the people with whom you interact are like germs—germs that have the power to transmit and infect. And life during this exceptional year can be quite taxing on your mental immune system to begin with, making you vulnerable to the attitudes around you. Just like you kept naysayers at bay when you planned your adventure, be picky about those you spend time with.

For good or for bad, I've had plenty of practice in dealing with toxic personalities, so I could spot them right away. Perhaps you know the type: They complain about everything; problems are always someone else's fault; and they are quick to gossip. Despite my own insecurity in a foreign land, I wasn't going to let myself get corralled into someone else's drama. So those were the times I let my Italian falter and didn't make the effort to connect.

For your part, choose happy, optimistic, and warm people while minimizing time with prickly, angry, and negative ones. At a minimum, be mindful of attitudes—including your own— so you can guide the situation and conversation in a healthier direction. Without such discernment and determination, you could be waking up on the wrong side of the bed too many of your 365 mornings, not knowing why.

Remember That Home Is Where You Are Living

Since you've uprooted yourself for a year, "home" may seem elusive—even more so if you are traveling around the world. Follow the "live in the present" mantra and try to define *home* as the "place where you are living." And use the word *home* with intention.

This means minimizing or eliminating references to "back home" defined as your native country. By doing this, you reduce the perceived distance between you and those you converse with in your host country. Words are powerful. And even something so trivial as using the word *home* judiciously can help foster stronger connection and friendship with those you meet.

During our year abroad, I trained myself to say "back in Portland" instead. There is a subtle distinction. The notion of home implies the warm, cozy place of belonging—and references to "back home" send the message that you don't belong where you *are*. Instead, let *home* refer to the place you're renting at the moment, even if you have to add qualifiers, such as "our apartment here in town." And train your mind to embrace the paradox that home can be both places at once: back home in your native land *and* wherever you live now.

Let's take this notion of fostering friendship by minimizing perceived distance one step further. You'll be inclined to voice comparisons of your adopted culture with your native culture, but try to avoid it unless people ask. They *will* ask, but you need not assault your hosts with a constant chorus of "back in the USA…"

BUILDING FRIENDSHIP WHILE TAKING ON A NEW LANGUAGE

It's a psychological workout to blend into the society of a new culture. When you add a non-native language to the mix, it's a workout of Olympic proportions.

No matter where you are on the spectrum of beginner to full fluency in a foreign tongue, to the locals you are an outsider. And though your goal isn't to blend in, being obviously Other while struggling with language can take its toll.

As someone who has studied Italian on and off for over twenty-five years, I had a solid grasp of the language when we arrived. But because I was the primary translator for our family, my brain was always shifting into high gear. So, whenever I entered the sanctuary of our home, I just wanted to chill—in English. This wasn't the dream I envisioned. We were supposed to be watching Italian TV together, struggling through commentary in our new adopted language. But that's not what happened.

Fortunately, outside of our English oasis we had plenty of opportunity to trip over mistakes as we strived to communicate in Italian. But despite the ongoing frustration with language learning, the rewards are rich. Sure, there's the whole second-language-is-good-for-your-brain thing or the what-a-gift-you-give-your-children thing. But in a paradoxical way your rudimentary speaking ability can facilitate a deeper, more authentic connection with others.

Your limited vocabulary in the moment forces you to think on your feet, using basic "primary color" words. Or it requires searching your dictionary app for that single incisive word to express the tone, shade, and intensity you mean to convey. And *how* you express yourself, along with the emotions you put into it, will have much more weight because you won't have the subtleties down. When I declined Simona's invitation with the simple "We're tired" statement, it was communicated with my whole body. She saw my unmistakable exhaustion.

This blunt style of communication can be plenty frustrating, but it quickly lets you convey your filter-free no-BS you. And while you may not care so much to offer a connection to your deeper, rawer self when buying vegetables, it helps in building friendships.

Think back to the second grade, when you had a rudimentary vocabulary and little understanding of complex emotions. Your friendships were heartfelt and authentic despite their sheer simplicity. The same thing happens when developing foreign-language skills in the classroom of your community abroad.

From the moment we saw Nicola and Laura holding up a welcome sign at the school kick-off picnic, the kindling of friendship sparked. Their daughter Cate was in Mattea's class, and English-speaking Nicola and my husband, Nick, got along famously. But Laura's Italian-only communication skills meant I had to find those points of connection and create a bond.

I liked her right away, and we had plenty in common: a deep interest in psychology, a curiosity about spirituality, even past careers in the entertainment industry. My steep and slow learning curve in building my Italian vocabulary in those subjects meant that to connect with Laura, I had to be at once vulnerable and blunt right from the beginning.

Laura learned stuff about my childhood that prompt ongoing analysis about my family of origin. She understands my fears of failure as a mom. She gets why I'm both drawn to and repelled by the Catholic church. And I think I even told her why I left an earlier career in television: because my ego wasn't cut out for all the egos I worked with. The self-protective measures I was so adept at weaving into conversation in English were tossed out the window for the sake of simple, genuine connection—one that Laura clearly wanted too.

Not everyone has the patience to deal with a language learner—just like not everyone was your bestie in the second grade. Plenty of folks will weed themselves out of your friendship sphere. Those who tickle with curiosity about you, who genuinely like you, who want to spend time with you, remain standing. Then it's up to you to welcome and cultivate friendships.

Growing your speaking ability still plays a big part in developing your friendships, however. And because language learning has been a big theme in my life, I've reflected on what has and hasn't worked in the past. Here are my biggest takeaways for a successful year abroad with a new language.

Don't Be Afraid to Make Mistakes

In fact, embrace them. This is how you learn. It's a tough pill to swallow if you have any perfectionist DNA. But, really, just get over it. Take a lesson from my husband, Nick, who is gifted with the ability to transform personal embarrassment into collective laughter.

One day in Genoa we were hanging out with friends in a large piazza crowded with food stands. Among the visual and olfactory delights calling us was a stand filled with fresh pastries. A particular biscotti stuffed with fresh fig was shouting Nick's name.

Because he's the outgoing, fearless type, Nick had no problem ordering in his caveman Italian. In fact, he had gotten by much of our time in Italy by adding an "a" or "o" to regular English words—which works for many nouns (stomach = *stomaco*; music = *musica*; problem = *problema*, etc.).

By now, Nick was even learning some finer points of translation, such as knowing that "fig" wasn't simply *figo* but rather that the "g" is replaced with a "c." But instead of ordering *biscotti di fico*, he ordered *biscotti di fica*, which promptly transformed the smiling face of the lady behind the counter into one of horror.

Thanks to our friend Silvia, who jumped in to save the day, the woman did not take offense that Nick was ordering a sack of [vulgar term for female genitalia] cookies. Everyone laughed heartily, all blushing aside. One of many such fearless-mistake incidents, this one ensures that Nick will forever read and *correctly* interpret any Italian menu listing fig as an ingredient.

Set Up Rules Regarding Conversation Exchange

With little effort you can find a conversation buddy, someone who will trade time teaching you the finer points of their native tongue while you reciprocate by offering English practice. No matter how formal (or informal) your arrangement, any practice in your target language with a native speaker willing to offer feedback is valuable. Before you start, though, make sure you each answer this simple question: To correct or not to correct?

The push-and-pull of wanting to be corrected when you make mistakes versus wanting to just practice communicating in your new language looms large. Setting rules around this is a key to success. I share what my wise Italian teacher, Gianluca, shared with me: Find someone who won't stop to correct you but rather will echo *correctly* what you're trying to say. He explained that the constant or even sporadic pointing out of mistakes undermines flow and erodes confidence. The idea that you're filing things away to later improve your skills is an illusion.

I've gone down both the "correct me" and "don't correct me" paths and can attest that Gianluca's advice is right on. You might set ground rules such as "Correct me *only* if I am going to embarrass myself or others" (à la the *fica* debacle) and "Please show me the correct way to say something by weaving it into our conversation." You might also consider setting parameters regarding time allotment, schedule, etc. Establish rules at the beginning of your arrangement, because once you get into a rhythm with someone, shifting gears becomes difficult.

Budget for Formal Lessons

Group classes are a fantastic way to learn a foreign language if you're a beginner or in a cohort of students at a similar level of proficiency. But if you hope to make large strides in a shorter amount of time, pony up for one-on-one lessons. For either, an experienced, skillful teacher is worth every penny.

You may not have a ton of options when looking for a good language school. But if you do, shop around. Look at their materials. They should grab you. A robust school typically offers film nights, excursions, and a variety of social events. A big bonus is you're likely to meet people from all over the world who are learning the same target language. This opens doors for more connections and future travel, and touches upon the essence of why you're living abroad.

Watch TV, Go to Movies, Listen to Music

Not only is such media in your target language a window onto the culture, they offer subliminal lessons. Reject those messages you heard growing up, such as "Turn off the TV!" "What is that ridiculous music?" "It's turning your brain to mush!" (or maybe that was just my family…).

Instead, enjoy the guiltless pleasure of watching whatever dumb TV you want to watch. It will increase your familiarity with your new language and passively lift you to greater proficiency.

ℓℓℓ

While you're learning a new language in your community abroad, it's best to check your expectations at the door. Know it will be rough, but it gets easier. You'll reach a point where your native English and your budding foreign vocabulary are a tangled mess in your mind. When the English word for something escapes you, take it as a good sign! After a time, you'll have the thrill of recounting a story and not remembering which language you originally heard it in.

Knowing another language is a gift that brings pleasure long after your adventure ends. It lets you weave your special year into your regular life, giving it a texture and richness that wasn't there before. Arriving here is worth every bump on the road.

BECOME PART OF THE COMMUNITY BY GIVING BACK

Despite your progress at building friendships, there will be times when you feel alien and adrift. The best antidote for such loneliness is to get involved in your community. This makes your entire experience abroad more human, and not one of passing through an anthropological zoo for an extended visit.

One approach to community participation is to think of it as giving back. And I don't mean with money or by shopping your way around the world to boost foreign economies. But, rather, by involving your mind, body, and spirit in helping the people of your host country in some decisive way. Such giving back is far more meaningful—and more rewarding for the giver too.

It won't take much to find a way to get involved. Whether it's asking around for a charity that needs volunteers or meandering into a house of worship, it's pretty easy to find a welcoming group.

For example, we visited the synagogue in Genoa, curious to learn about its history and wanting to ask where we could purchase Hanukkah candles in uber-Catholic Italy. After a twenty-minute visit with some folks who worked there, it became clear we could have an instant network of people, eager to provide plenty of opportunity for involvement. Though we weren't drawn to that call, it's an example of how easily the door swings open.

If your year abroad includes children, look no further than their school for a wide scope of prospects for contributing. Far from being pure altruism, giving back at school offers benefits too:

- Your kids experience more belonging when they see you involved.
- You get to know fellow parents, teachers, and your kids' classmates.
- You get an inside view of your kids' daily school activity.

As a foreigner, your involvement at a local school has instant educational appeal. If you're living in a non-English-speaking country, exposure to your native tongue will be a hot commodity. This is how we chose to offer our time—teaching English. And full confession: It wasn't always easy, nor did we always look forward to it. But it was undeniably rewarding, for us *and* for the kids we taught.

Nick and I spent hours researching games and lessons for young English learners, which we delivered twice a month. The chance to get creative, use multimedia, and exercise our leadership and presentation muscles boosted the reward. And as we played ambassador for kids who might never step foot in North America, we developed a newfound respect for the teaching profession (wrangling twenty-plus kids is not easy). We are still in touch with those teachers and several students, the ripples of our efforts still palpable.

If you're reluctant to commit to an ongoing project, random opportunities may still turn up. In her book, *Il Bel Centro: A Year in the Beautiful Center*, Michelle Damiani describes her family's participation in the annual Spello Flower Festival. During their year abroad, the Damianis delightfully accepted an invitation to join a neighborhood team for the *infiorata,* wherein local Italians make pictorial carpets from flowers, blanketing the entire village in a stunning explosion of colors.

The weeks of planning and hands-on involvement in something so rooted in Spello's history was a visceral highlight of the Damianis' experience overseas. Passive observation of the beautiful festival would certainly have presented colorful memories, but it wouldn't have come close to their memories of being actively involved.

LEND HANDS AROUND THE WORLD

If your planned adventure is one of continuous travel, opportunities to participate in community can still be found in abundance. And going to the effort of finding them will color and shape your adventure. Here's some further insight into how Jen Shafer and Tracey Carisch managed their community building while traveling.

Jen Shafer, who spent the better part of a year traveling overseas with her partner, Patrick, stresses that her time working with local farmers and on public service projects was "absolutely priceless." They planned their travels in conjunction with volunteer opportunities. Their journey included Europe, Morocco, two months in Turkey, six in Southeast Asia, a month hiking the Annapurna mountain range in central Nepal, and nearly three months in Australia and beyond.

Jen recounts her experience doing "voluntourism" overseas firsthand: "We lived in their neighborhoods, which we never would have visited otherwise. We enjoyed meals at their tables, where we learned so much about local culture, politics, and life in general from their perspective. We saved a lot of money by volunteering while we traveled. This was a big driver at first, but it ended up being our preferred mode of travel, money savings or not. Being a tourist is so boring after a while!"

Lest you think that kind of freedom and flexibility is only possible without kids, Tracey and Brian Carisch did a very similar thing with three kids in tow (ages eleven, eight, and six). Their approach was to shape-shift a computer engineering job to work remotely while plotting their route by way of service projects. Like Jen and Patrick, they lined up some volunteering opportunities ahead of time, and were often welcomed by smiling faces upon their arrival. But, more frequently than not, they stumbled into their projects, learning about opportunities in random places such as cafés and town markets.

The Carisch kids got involved too, doing a variety of things from farmwork to cooking to childcare. Tracey recalls that some of their most memorable projects involved offering up her and Brian's professional skills, as they helped organizations with strategic planning, technology issues, and even photography for marketing materials. Their efforts aided people and groups from Ireland to Peru; Ethiopia to Cambodia; Thailand to New Zealand—and plenty of places in between.

Fueled by the powerful Why of wanting to change the world in small ways, the Carisches managed this lifestyle for eighteen months before returning to the US. Read more about Tracey's experience in her book, *Excess Baggage: One Family's Around-the-World Search for Balance.*

And if you're wondering how you might weave voluntourism into your adventure, even if it's not the overarching theme of your adventure, take a page from their playbook. Like Jen, you can plug into a broad geographic network such as Worldwide Opportunities on Organic Farms (www.wwoof.net) or Global Village (www.habitat.org/gv) and plan your travels around the available possibilities. (Learn more from Jen's "Travel Resources" at slowlyglobal.blogspot.com.) Or you can mix it up like the Carisches did, always having your eyes open for a need to fill.

The common denominator and key ingredient is *intent.* As long as you nurture the intent to give back, the opportunities will present themselves.

$$\ell\ell\,$$

Whether you live in a single place for the duration of your adventure or are continually on the move, your experience will be far richer if you find a way to participate in local efforts. Not only will you create colorful memories, but you'll cultivate relationships and weave yourself into the fabric of a community.

At a minimum, participation in community offers you a front-row seat to the culture. And you'll no doubt receive plenty of invitations from locals. Say yes as often as you can. Whether you partake in a local festival, volunteer at school, or simply accept and reciprocate dinner invitations, go for it. With gusto.

COMMUNITY BACK HOME

While we're on the topic of community, let's not forget the one you left behind in your native country. If you plan to return to your same network, wending back into its rhythm is a big part of the process. And while you're away, keeping your connections alive goes a long way in easing back into your *new* old life.

Though it may seem like a chore, maintaining a blog (see Chapter 7) is an easy way to stay connected to home—when done in an authentic voice. You might be tempted to put only your airbrushed lives out there and barrage your friends with pretty pictures and "happy life" posts, but that gets old and off-putting after a while. While you don't have to share your lowest lows (lice, anyone?), aim to be true. Let your friends and family in on your real life. Include the downs with the ups. The same holds true no matter what form of social media you use.

More power to you if you choose to travel back to the twentieth century and shun the bulk of digital technology while you're abroad. But try to keep a lifeline to your previous world. Donate to that annual school fundraiser you'll gladly be skipping while you're overseas. Contribute a note to your work or neighborhood newsletter back home. Send your annual holiday greeting. However minimal, make sure a tentacle or two still reaches the community you left behind.

It's also an option to go radio silent for the year. And perhaps that's the healthiest choice for your life. But know that reentry will be starkly different if you've been 100 percent out of sight and mind with those back home.

ellee

SAVE IT FOR SOMEDAY TIPS

- If you have a strong sense that your adventure abroad will involve a language you aren't comfortable speaking, then work on proficiency. Yes, I'm a nag with the language thing. You'll thank me later.

- If you envision any part of your year abroad doing volunteer work with an established international group, such as Habitat for Humanity, explore your options sooner rather than later. Figure out which group fits you best. Once you find a good fit, it could go a long way in helping shape your adventure, even furnishing some crucial connections to make it happen.
- If you have a sense for the kind of giving back you'll delight in doing, get some practice. It's one thing to say you'll volunteer in a classroom and a whole other thing to be in a room trying to hold the interest of twenty-five children!

CHAPTER NINE

TAKE CARE OF YOU

IF WE WERE TO look at symbolic representation of your year abroad coming into reality, it would involve a lot of arrows protruding from you as a stick figure. Think about all the outward projection you need to do: seek *out* sources of information you don't have; reach *out* to strangers; exit your country to go *across* a border, etc.

You've harnessed your courage to be shot out of a cannon to follow the arc of your trajectory—and then you're plopped down in a new part of the world, waiting for the ringing in your ears to stop. Except that doesn't happen because all this amazing stimuli continues to assault and delight the senses.

Where are *you* in this picture? The *you* that needs self-nurturing time to recharge? Ditto for anyone you've brought along on the journey. How can *they* nurture themselves at *their* core?

The simple answer for taking care of the heart of you is to give yourself plenty of time and protect your space—as much as you're able.

This chapter covers what that might look like for the you who's in a unique situation, living as a stranger in a strange land, where previous best practices in self-care may not apply.

GIFT YOURSELF MORE TIME

Once you land abroad, it may be tempting to hit the ground running because your engine is revved up. Resist this at first. It's not a Formula One race. The whole point of taking such an extended period away is precisely so you don't have to race across your destined route.

Instead, take a moment to catch your breath. Perhaps that moment is only a day or two if you're roaming the planet. Or maybe it's a week or two if you've moved to that one special place for the year. And it doesn't mean you do nothing during this period—but rather that you aren't being consumed by an agenda. Let yourself ease into a new rhythm.

Also, remember that many regular tasks will take longer than usual. What might've taken you twenty minutes back home (because you know the ropes) could turn into a three-hour odyssey as you navigate language, maps, public transit, and all things unfamiliar. If you end up not needing the extra stretch allotted, that's bonus time for you!

PACE YOURSELF AND PRIORITIZE

As you researched *and* planned your adventure, a loose set of must-sees and must-dos no doubt formed. And then as your year abroad unfolds, more must-sees and must-dos come into view. When you add in probable visitors and unexpected opportunities that present themselves, your calendar gets crowded pretty quickly. The key to surviving while thriving is to pace yourself and prioritize.

I'm reminded of a rhyme my dad would say when we'd dine at a favorite local cafeteria: "Don't eat like a pelican, where your eyes eat more than your belly can." When plotting and planning how you envision the adventure year, everything you read about becomes a must-see, and in your imagination it's doable. But in reality that bucket list is achievable only if you run on fumes and schedule little to no sleep. Like the array of mouth-watering cafeteria options, the "belly" can only hold so much.

Even if you're the rare breed that finds it exhilarating to be intensely busy, remember two things: You may not get to it all, and your priorities will shift during your year.

Take this example of priorities shifting: Your former fraternity brother is eager to organize a weeklong reunion in Baja. Before you embarked on your big adventure, this sounded like a blast. But now that your family has settled into a relaxed Costa Rican rhythm, you dread the disruption it will mean.

Here's another scenario: You overestimated your energy reserves and find yourself wanting to cancel the big trip to Colombia you've been planning for months. And when you try to pinpoint why you feel so drained, you realize it's that obligatory fraternity reunion trip that has been weighing you down!

If it's not second nature to pace yourself and prioritize, then prompt a look inward. Tune in to your energy levels. Get familiar with the warning signs of early exhaustion. Learn to recognize when an idea or activity increases your energy because it brings you *joy* versus drains your energy out of some sense of obligation.

This wasn't easy for us, and I can't say we succeeded. Too often we had the looming thought, "But we need to take advantage of our situation. We *should* go to France this weekend. It's not *that* far." But by the time the weekend rolled around, we could barely muster the energy to take the train to the local park in Nervi. It took far too many months to understand and *own* our limited capacity to get up and go.

The more skilled you become at tuning in, the more honest you can be with others, and with yourself. Then it's easier to avoid doing things out of mere obligation. And it becomes second nature to prioritize and schedule life at a reasonable pace.

PROTECT YOUR SPACE

Whether you focus your aim to "take care of you" or "tune in to self-awareness," one of the best things to do is protect your space. While locks and bolts on your physical space are a good idea, I'm talking about your mental and emotional space. The simple intention to keep healthy margins of mental and emotional space supports your well-being. It also supports the well-being of your relationships, especially with those who accompany you on this journey.

Your Mental Space

You likely have a daily media diet of some sort. Maybe it's the traditional morning news digest over coffee, listening to the radio during your commute, or social media checks throughout the day. Whether as a friend or a follower, you have your finger on the pulse of your culture.

Fast-forward to your leap past the border to another culture. Your information diet will change by necessity. At a minimum, your rhythm for intake will change. Not only might regular access to Wi-Fi be sparse, but finding your favorite nondigital newspaper or magazine, much less getting it delivered without extra time or cost, will be next to impossible.

Once you consider all the new fun things entering your sphere, will you *want* to keep up with your usual politics or a never-ending Twitter/Facebook/Instagram feed? I'm betting on no! You can try, but it'll only divide your presence between *there* and where you *are*.

One of the most freeing things for me during my year abroad was to cut off my usual news intake. That's not to say I buried my head in the sand, but instead I got my news from an Italian or a European perspective, which in and of itself was plenty insightful. I also limited Facebook activity and emails back home. It was hard enough to stay caught up with Italian school-related exchanges for my kids. At the absolute bottom of my list of welcome activities was more computer time.

And I must confess, it was delightfully liberating not to be wound up in the latest drama between Congress and the president, or which movies had been nominated for an Oscar. By being less in touch with American culture, I could become more European while I was away.

While you are away, I encourage you to disconnect from the ever-present cloud of "North America Think." Doing so gives you a margin of clean mental space that offers the freedom to be in the here and now, wherever that may be. This doesn't mean cutting yourself off from friends and family; rather, give yourself the power to choose when, how much, and how often to stay in touch.

Your Emotional Space with Family

I've touched upon how 24/7 together time can be overwhelming early on during the year abroad. But as your odyssey gets underway, you'll learn each other's rhythms so deeply that it redefines *tight-knit*. And I mean that in a good way.

The initial period post-leap when it's all family, all the time can be a carnival of horrors. It's messy—like when you first plunge your clean hands into a pile of dough that needs mixing. You want to avoid the mess that gets stuck in the crevices of your fingers and nails. But then it becomes kind of pleasurable, even fun, as you start to shape the culinary delight you're making. You just go with it.

Amy Maroney, author of the Miramonde series, describes the bond her family created during their time overseas as "superglue." That superglue was so powerful that they still refer to their sabbatical several years later. Similarly, my family refers to our collective life as "Before Italy" and "After Italy" because that year was so defining. I remember thinking during our time overseas, "I *thought* I knew my kids, but boy was I wrong." Such an intense shared experience brought closeness to a whole new level.

Your Emotional Space with Your Partner

Be aware that the intensity can also take its toll on your spousal relationship. Whatever emotional space you've grown accustomed to with your partner, expect to be disoriented—even with something as simple as going out together. For example, back home in Portland, Nick and I were disciplined about getting a date night at least twice a month. In Italy, I don't think we even had two dates over the course of our twelve months there!

This was a huge fail on our part, one we would rectify if we could have a do-over. It's easy to attribute our laziness about taking a romantic evening out to not knowing a babysitter or not wanting to stress out our kids. But it was a shoulda, coulda, woulda of epic proportion. If you embark on this journey with young kids, please don't repeat our mistake. Experience your adventure every so often through the romantic eyes of a couple. It will add a texture and depth you won't get otherwise.

Protecting the emotional space you share with your partner is not about marriage survival, though at times it might feel that way. Rather, the challenges arising from doing a year abroad strengthen any relationship that stands on solid ground. But if your relationship is *not* on solid ground, take heed. Consider meeting with a therapist in advance of your departure to learn some tools and/or set some rules for when difficulty creeps up— because it *will.*

And Your Own Space

When taking care of your family's emotional space, often the most overlooked relationship is the one you have with yourself.

Family togetherness can spill over the brim, leaving you to run from the flood. And you *should* run on occasion—to protect your sanity *and* your family togetherness. The wise old adage "absence makes the heart grow fonder" rings true.

Schedule regular solo time (and not just to run to the market) that allows you to reenter the familial sphere with a happy face. And if you opt to homeschool, reread that last sentence and underscore it. In fact, every member of your household would do well to nurture his or her personal "margin" in order to nurture your collective relationships.

Visitors and Your Welcome Mat

The one area where protecting your space is meant in the literal sense is when your space is at risk for invasion—by *visitors*.

As soon as you announce your set plans to go abroad for a while, friends, family, and acquaintances alike will toss out feelers for visiting you. Sure, they could be just daydreaming out loud. But because you are following through on this leave-the-country dream, it emboldens and encourages others to jump on board.

Acquaintances may tell you how they've always wanted to travel to your target location, "so wouldn't it be great if we did it while you're there!" Jet-setter colleagues may fancy a visit since they have plans to be "in the area," which for them might mean the same hemisphere. And don't forget the family and close friends who can't bear the thought of being apart for a whole year.

Sure, you'll want to welcome them all while showing off your tour-guide skills. But be forewarned that the fun factor is much higher when the travel plans are theoretical. I am your future self traveling back in time to tell you:

- Less is more.
- Don't bite off more than you can chew.
- Dole out your invitations with intention!

Just like the aforementioned fraternity brother who plans a big reunion in your neck of the woods, be careful about what you commit to. This includes being too vague about *not* committing to something. (Saying no can be hard!) Protect your space by not overextending yourselves.

Only a fraction of folks who express interest in visiting you will follow through, but you might be surprised at who shows up at your doorstep. (Just as you might be equally surprised at who *doesn't* make the effort to stay connected.) So when leading up to your launch overseas, don't throw out a "Come visit us!" to everyone, unless you're okay with becoming a revolving door for couch-surfing friends.

For those visitors who *do* jump through the hoops to piggyback on your adventure, stay mindful to preserve your margin. Perhaps, like us, you won't be able to accommodate visitors due to a small apartment, thereby maintaining your breathing room. Or you'll have self-sufficient, savvy travelers who are easy to manage. Best rule of thumb: Fit guests into *your* rhythm and not the other way around.

And for any visitors who need a lot of hand-holding, set mutual expectations. Make sure everyone is on the same page with expenses, food preferences, sleep habits, and activity levels.

While you sync up expectations, don't neglect to sync up schedules too. Visitors tend to cluster around school schedules and holidays, which might limit your own family's flexibility and freedom during the one year you should have plenty of both. Amy of the "superglue" family loved seeing family and friends but cautions against scheduling too many visits far in advance. I wish I had gotten her wise advice earlier, because, predictably, as our year in Italy progressed, our energy reserves were depleting. And a flock of friends had long scheduled their visit during our eleventh month, leaving no rest for our weary selves!

With every aspect of protecting your space, aim to find a balance between the cost and reward. Remember, saying yes to others is often saying no to yourself, and vice versa.

A VACATION IS STILL A VACATION

Before we left for Europe, we naively thought that we were embarking on a thirteen-month-long vacation. We knew it wouldn't be a vacation in the traditional sense of the word, but we didn't anticipate that all the stressful life stuff would rear its ugly head as often as it did. Our saving grace was a commitment to a monthly getaway to explore our new corner of the world. And at some point midway through our year, we realized how necessary those getaways were. When it comes down to it, a vacation is still a vacation.

Don't be surprised if those back home deem you epic travelers and assume you're having the grand tour of a lifetime. If you hunker down in a single location, they'll project all the romance and fun of whatever exotic place you've chosen. Our current "put your best selfie forward" culture, along with travel magazines and TV shows that drive the tourism industry, exaggerate these perceptions. But in your little expat bubble, you're just living your life. A life that still benefits from—nay, *requires*—a break from routine.

We've already covered traveling in regard to the virtues of planning ahead versus being spontaneous (see Chapter 6). But consider this a reminder. With the effort you've made to get yourselves abroad, budget in the time and money for travel. It could end up being an unprecedented year of expenses. But unless you see frequent world travel in your future while still spry enough to get about, take this to heart: *You only live once and you may not pass this way again.* Harsh? Perhaps. Motivating? I hope so.

Our weekend jaunts to nearby villages or nearby countries on the continent took effort. But every time we escaped to someplace new, we returned refreshed and reminded of why we were doing this year abroad in the first place. While our new friends in Italy didn't know what to make of us, the girls' teachers understood that this was an exceptional period. Though we may have given the false impression of being jet-setters, we had no choice but to embrace it.

And if you're doing a 'round-the-world odyssey, then think of "vacation" as breaking from the routine. That could be as simple as dinner out at a rogue burger joint because you couldn't possibly do another rice dish this month. Or it could be about mixing up your activities.

If art and history museums are your usual go-to places, give the kids a day of fun and visit an amusement park, no matter how repulsive sticky candy-covered carnival rides might sound to you. If you are adventuring with social purpose, then fold in activities that are sheer self-indulgence. Or punctuate your delightful, dizzying nonstop tourism with days of book-reading calm.

The bottom line: Fold in periodic breaks in order to reset, recharge, and reengage with a fresh perspective. No matter what, *take care of you*. As long as you keep a firm handle on your time and your space—and encourage other family members to do the same—your year abroad will be a success by almost any measure.

eelee

SAVE IT FOR SOMEDAY TIPS

- Identify the best practices for taking care of yourself. What are your usual ways to de-stress? Does meditation help you maintain calm and focus? Cooking? Reading? Running? However you do it, know yourself so you'll have a go-to practice when needed. Encourage your family members to do the same.

- Learn to tune in to other peoples' energy and recognize when it feeds and supports you. Get good at navigating interpersonal dynamics so you foster more of that positive, supportive energy—and less negative, draining energy. This skill not only helps to make your year abroad fall into place as it should, but ensures that those who visit won't drag you down or trap you in a whirl of obligation.

- When you start to focus on a dream location, do passive research on what area travel might encompass. For example, if you think about Argentina as a possible target location, then tuck away any article or show about South American travel you find. When the time comes to plan excursions, you'll be better informed and able to cut to the chase. And as you sift through possibilities, keep your anticipated budget in mind. Drooling over luxury resorts is not worth the tease when you could be exploring affordable options.

CHAPTER TEN

GROW YOUR WINGS

BY THE TIME YOUR year abroad comes to a close, the familiar feelings of impending goodbyes and "Big Transition Ahead" take hold. Mixed feelings of sadness, excitement, and maybe even anxiety about what's next will come full circle as your adventure ends.

But it's different from your pre-adventure anticipation. *You're* different. Many moons away from the comfortable routine transforms a person. Maybe not to the dramatic extent of a caterpillar becoming a butterfly, but you *will* be a different you.

The big exit from your foreign odyssey also differs because you're returning to the familiar, not to a land of unexplored territory. Even if you relocate, like the Carisches did by moving to another state, or Loey Werking Wells and family did by virtue of having sold their house, you are reentering a familiar culture where you know the essential ropes.

But the biggest thing that makes this transition homeward exceptional is the power to reimagine your life because you created such a defining quest. You can enjoy a fresh start, not simply a retreat into your former life. While some retreating is inevitable, you'll move forward and integrate aspects of your newfound worldliness into your daily routine. You may have come full circle, but don't lift the pencil off the page just yet.

ALL GOOD THINGS MUST COME TO AN END

As the finish line comes into view, you enter a bit of a no-man's-land—in both an emotional and a practical way. You begin to organize logistics for a smooth trip back while you are forced to accept a basic truth: However you've integrated yourself into your community abroad, you're really just passing through. And for those who are finishing a 'round-the-world odyssey, your final destinations are just that—a destination before heading home.

Anticipating the Departure

With school in its final weeks, we were prepping for our departure while our adopted community was focused on plans for the season. My oldest daughter's classmates were all talking about their various *scuola media* selections. Summer vacation plans were being hatched as beach blankets and bathing suits were coming out. The world turned while we packed up. The stark reminder that we were just a ship in Genoa's port contrasted with the feelings of connection that had taken root.

I wanted to crawl out of my skin during our last month in Italy because I couldn't resolve my conflicted feelings. I did *not* want to leave. I dreaded the goodbyes, and I knew that tearing myself away from the comfort of my new home and new language would hurt like the proverbial bandage being ripped off.

Yet I looked forward to our meandering European exit and seeing the smiling faces of our friends in Germany and Norway— not to mention a joyful reunion with folks in the US. It was a lose-win situation. But during that final month in Italy, the lose side cast a large shadow over the win side.

The bittersweet feelings that swelled reminded me of those last weeks before graduation from high school, college, or even grade school. That complex period where one reflects on the challenges, triumphs, and friendships, as well as those notable teachers. Even the sights and smells of one's surroundings hit the olfactory nerve in a piercing way, bringing up the sadness of fleeting time tinged with excitement for the freedom of what comes next.

Handling the Emotional Chaos

So, how does one handle this paradoxical goodbye-hello situation? What else can you do but go through it and embrace it?

In many ways, this year of adventure becomes a microcosm of your life, and those death-bed questions creep up: Did I make it count? Did I work at my family and friend relationships? Did I embrace my deepest self, and learn what I'm all about? Did I maintain my balance and act with grace through the difficult moments?

Unlike the end of life, though, despite the year abroad chapter coming to a close, you get to write the next chapters going forward. What will you write, and how will it flow from your unique experience?

And though these philosophical questions may float around in your head, the finiteness of your year looms large. Before you realize it, every calendar day is filled with activities. They might include checking off a few sites you've been meaning to tour, a slew of packing and shipping tasks, or managing visitors who are squeezing in their trip before you leave.

Pressure mounts as things compress down at the narrow end of the funnel. The emotional chaos and the deeper musings about your year's takeaways get pushed aside as you sort through the practicalities of returning to your homeland.

PRACTICAL TIPS AS YOU PREPARE YOUR EXIT
As you organize your pending departure, take advantage of my 20/20 hindsight:

- Don't overbook yourselves. And if for some crazy reason you must entertain visitors at the end of your adventure, set them up to be independent so you don't have to hand-hold them.
- Leave space for the small but important tasks like making sure you have gifts for folks back home. Even buying a bunch of generic souvenirs can chew up hours. Better yet, acquire gifts throughout the year. Be those annoying Christmas shoppers who have everything purchased and wrapped months before.
- Be sure you gather any necessary documents from your community abroad, such as school transcripts, while it's still easy to do.
- Get a jump on making appointments in your native home ahead of your arrival, such as dental cleaning, pediatric checkups, and so forth—especially if your providers book up far in advance.
- Don't wait till the last minute to pack or ship your belongings. Organize, and avoid panic mode so your stuff doesn't become a burden precisely when you'd rather spend time with the people in your lives. Give away things that aren't precious to you. Most times, it's cheaper to buy new things upon your return than pay to ship them back. (Tip: If you do ship some things internationally, if possible label contents as "used personal items," which should speed up any customs inspections.)

And for those who enjoyed the bulk of their experience in one location:

- Be sure to visit your favorite shops, cafés, and other

202 | LET'S LEAVE THE COUNTRY!

sites. You'll want to offer a deliberate goodbye to the friendly faces you've come to know over the year.

- Plan some kind of farewell gathering for the friends you've made. Stealth departures cheat everyone from much-needed closure.

ele

The crush of these last weeks harkens back to those weeks before you embarked on this epic undertaking. So, whatever you can do to simplify the process is key to maintaining a semblance of balance—and enough margin for "goodbye."

NAVIGATING THE JOURNEY HOME

Given how long you've been gone, and the geographic distance of your location abroad, consider taking the long way home. Just as a scuba diver who ascends too quickly can get the bends, a day of plane travel may not be sufficient to soften the blow of being plopped down exactly where your journey began a year before. This is particularly true if you've been living in a single location as opposed to having a 'round-the-world experience.

I encourage you to buffer your homecoming with some old-fashioned travel. Even the zoo travel you've avoided thus far is a welcome way to amble homeward, decompressing as you go. In our case, we meandered through Europe before getting on a plane in London. The Vaughns wrapped up their adventure in Argentina by tacking on a vacation to Brazil *and* a regional road trip in the US so their renters back home could finish out their lease.

Another way to ease that transition is to choose a slower trans-portation method. Harper and Andrew, who lived in England for a couple of years with their two children, decided they would travel home to the US vintage-style—by boat. Though the cruise ship ride took seven days instead of seven hours, it was a crucial week when they could mentally prepare for their bittersweet homecoming.

However you manage it, an extended return trip allows you and your family to cocoon a bit, apart from an active community. Cocooning is a natural reaction as you process all you've been through over the previous twelve months. And prepare for it to continue even after you arrive home.

EVERYTHING OLD IS NEW AGAIN

The longer you're away from home, the bigger and stronger are the waves that reverberate from reverse culture shock. In a way, it's kind of fun—akin to emerging from a sensory deprivation tank. Your fresh, acute senses greet a bright, loud, and pungent world. But make no mistake, it can be quite jarring.

Even though you might lessen the jolt of reentry by taking the slow road, you still won't be able to eliminate the shock. Your homecoming prompts a reckoning similar to the sensory overload you experienced when you began your year abroad. And because this awe doesn't last (you *will* reacclimate), take notes—even if you're not the introspective type. Trust me, people will bombard you with questions about your experience, your highs and your lows, and what it feels like to be home. It's more fun for everyone if you have thoughtful answers.

As soon as you land on your native turf, a series of firsts begin: your first transaction with native currency; your first true native meal; your first car trip on native soil. And so on. Relish the foreignness as you see everything in a stark new light.

From the moment our plane touched down, and throughout the journey home, it struck me how new the buildings and roads were relative to those in Europe. Our feet had grown accustomed to navigating sixteenth-century walk-streets and taking in the patina of wind-worn palazzos. Now, nothing built before 1940 crossed our path as we zoomed over smooth tar-covered pavement in an oversized taxicab.

I remember being paralyzed in the supermarket, trying to select a tub of yogurt from the gazillion options. Back in Genoa, I would delight in finding a simple Greek yogurt at the store. But here we have giant supermarkets! Endless choices! Lots of helpful clerks! I was like a deer in headlights, and I knew if I didn't pick up the pace I'd spend half the day shopping for three bags of groceries.

Based on my unscientific survey of expats returning to the US, typical reentry impressions echo mine. And they include all sorts of insights on how big everything is—the people, the cars, the houses, the roads, the meal portions. That may be no surprise, but it still doesn't hold a candle to experiencing reverse culture shock firsthand. So absorb it with deep appreciation.

GETTING YOUR SEA LEGS

After the initial homecoming shock dissipates, don't expect to just pick up where you left off. A good night's sleep, or several, doesn't do the trick either. The adjustment period before getting fully settled in to your native culture is akin to being in a decompression chamber after deep-sea diving. Though your body might be over jet lag, there's no shame in accessing your cocoon whenever the need to retreat arises.

Think about it: You've been away for a yearlong stretch of being pulled and twisted like taffy while experiencing the marvel of fresh new vistas. And now you're back to your old life. Which is really your new—and dare I say *better*—life. You're wise to anticipate a period of metamorphosis or gestation until you fully reemerge.

And, to be clear, everyone will have a unique homecoming experience. You might luck into having perfectly calm weather, both internally and externally, such that your issues are minimal. But, for most people, becoming fully acclimated again takes time.

How Long Does It Take?

Steve Meyers and Ryanne Rothenberg, who spent three years in Phuket, Thailand, said it took almost two years to reacclimate to life in the US. Laura Ligabue, who spent six months in London before returning to her native Italy, needed three months in her cocoon. The deeper (and longer) you climb into a culture, the steeper (and longer) the climb out will be.

There's emotional adjustment, but there's social and physical adjustment too—for example, something as simple as your gut getting used to local foods again. Everyone's process period is different, even within a single family. Kids tend to rebound more quickly.

Our younger daughter, Mattea, hit the ground running as soon as she reconnected with friends, while Chiara reengaged more slowly. My husband lagged behind them by several months, while I needed still more processing time.

Despite any needed adjustment, life moves on, and rather quickly at that. To your friends and family, you will walk and talk like the same people you were before you left. And assuming you kept a blog or sent out regular updates, they will have followed your journey with you. But unless you also followed blogs and updates from those back home, you won't be on the same page. The mutual feeling of being caught up and informed will be lopsided at best.

The conversations that ensue might require extra focus on your part. Be prepared to repeat the same stories for months, and to ask the same questions over and over again. As you get up to speed in your social circles, keeping track almost requires a spreadsheet, which can be exhausting in its own right.

The Lived-Abroad Club

While you reacclimate, you may crave connection with those who have been through a comparable transition. It is a treasure to engage with others who lived where you did, or who went through a similar year abroad experience. If you don't know such folks in your community, there's no shortage of resources online to access good company if you feel the need (search terms: repatriation + expats + return + "reverse culture shock").

ℓℓℓ

Support yourself however works best as you readjust, because before you know it, your new old life becomes routine again. And while you won't get from zero to sixty in a week, others might expect that. So be firm about setting your own pace, adjusting as needed. And ask yourself, What speed do I want to accelerate *to*?

ABOUT THOSE WINGS

After your amazing expedition, returning to an environment that may have changed only incrementally should be a piece of cake. But dramatic change *has* happened—inside of *you*. And the challenge of reassimilating a new and improved you into the familiarity of your old stomping ground is a tremendous gift. As you ease out of your cocoon, your budding wings allow you to attain a higher perspective on your horizon. This time, you decide what that life looks like.

If you return to your same job, what could you change to make it more ideal? If you hunt for a new job, what would suit you *better* than the old one? You've spent the last couple of years moving a mountain to create the adventure of a lifetime, followed by navigating all kinds of delightful and anxiety-provoking unknowns. This counts for something. Don't deny your newfound superpowers. They can help you maneuver the ins and outs of making desired changes happen.

And if no sweeping changes are in order, what about smaller ones? If nothing else, the year abroad trains you in subtle and not-so-subtle ways of looking out for yourself. No doubt you'll gain a keener awareness of human dynamics or develop a finer inner compass about how you best shine. Use them to your advantage. There's no better occasion to establish new rhythms than during those first months of getting resituated.

In my case, after returning home I was very choosy when it came to accepting invitations—especially when those invitations involved a lot of my precious time. Instead of saying yes to most of those school volunteer requests, I would let others jump in. I vowed that my saying no would be a guilt-free way of saying yes to myself.

It became a priority to fold the slower Italian pace into my American life. Italians are notorious for going at a leisurely pace (even when a quicker one is warranted!). While living there, I got over my annoyance at their languor and embraced the slower pace. Now, a few years later, it might take me several days to respond to some emails, which was unheard of before Italy. As for the other things I'd hoped to adopt, such as improving my culinary skills, or walking more instead of driving, I still have a way to go… But hey, now I have goals!

And while the kinds of changes I'm talking about are possible for *anyone,* sabbatical or not, making that grand exit and reentry after an epic adventure can put a magic fire in your belly. Such experience and reflections combine to create a new set of empowerment tools to aid in your transformation.

The area of friendships illustrates this. No doubt that during your extended time away you'll crave being able to converse using the carefree, informal language between friends (even more so if you didn't live in an English-speaking country). After returning home, you'll revel in the abundance of free and easy conversation, but you'll also reflect on the friends you made overseas. Ask yourself if parts of you were able to be more authentic when you were deprived of all your normal social trappings. If so, aim at folding that authenticity into all your established relationships.

Hopefully, the sabbatical experience will yield plenty of opportunity for you to understand your deeper self, as it did for me.

However, expressing those newfound aspects of yourself among people who know only the "old" you is not without its challenges. Take advantage of this restart to get a firmer grip on your steering wheel. Allow yourself to navigate with fresh eyes as you hold onto a newly defined, albeit vulnerable, you.

Continuing the Adventure Back Home

And what about the life you left overseas? What do you miss? What from your travels or your adopted culture would you like to incorporate into your reestablished lifestyle?

Those new-grown wings can fly you back whenever you want, figuratively speaking, of course. With some intention, it's easy to:

- Cook favorite meals from your year abroad (so be sure to collect recipes!).
- Listen to music that transports you to your year abroad.
- Watch films or TV from your adopted country.
- Keep your new language going if you went to a non-English-speaking country. Music and media help, but seek opportunities to practice speaking, particularly if you have kids who gained proficiency.
- Connect with people who lived in the country you did, or who had a similar experience as yours.
- Create art using materials you bring back. Not only is it therapeutic, you'll end up with visuals to remind you of your eye-popping adventure. If making art is not for you, then frame your favorite photos, or put up any art you purchased during your travels.
- Continue to cultivate your friendships from overseas. Just as you made the effort to keep in touch with friends back home while you were gone, do the same now with any good friends you made abroad. These people connections, more than anything, are what

keep the year abroad alive—and set you up for future visits with your foreign friends, either here or in your adopted country. Don't be the annoying person who goes radio silent and then hopes for a big welcome during a future visit.

And be on guard for excessive rose-colored retro-vision. Your desire to keep the year abroad relevant may result in painful nostalgic moments from time to time. If they're too much to bear, use reverse psychology on yourself. Think of something you missed terribly when you were overseas—whether it's a meal, an activity, or spending time with a particular friend. And then savor every moment while you experience that thing.

ели

Whether you lived in a single location and can call a distant foreign place another home or you drank in a rich experience from around the world, you have added a unique texture to your life. Don't let that disappear.

At some point you may yearn to visit your home abroad. Or perhaps a dozen months of exploratory travel have planted a seed of wanderlust you can't ignore.

In whatever way you hear the winds calling you, ask yourself how this experience redefined you, and how you want to redefine the life ahead of you. Pondering such questions may just bring you to the foothills of your next adventure, however it unfolds!

елее

SAVE IT FOR SOMEDAY TIPS

Let's come full circle. After reading this book, do you still dream of living abroad for a while?

- If your answer is a resounding *yes*, go back to page 1 and throw yourself into the process. You *can* make it happen.
- If so, but you're still intimidated by it, get in touch with that Why—the Why of your intimidation as well as the Why of your desire to go.
- If, on the other hand, you're confident regular vacation-style travel will be good enough for you, that's an enormous piece of self-knowledge to own. Perhaps there is another mountain you could climb.

Whatever your dream, go make it happen.

IN BOCCA AL LUPO

IN ITALY, INSTEAD OF wishing someone "good luck" (or *buona fortuna*), one says, "*In bocca al lupo*," which means "in the mouth of the wolf." The correct response to this is not "*grazie*" (thank you) but "*crepi il lupo*," which means "may the wolf die."

In bocca al lupo, according to many Italians, proffers the wish that when you face a scary challenge, you will conquer it (instead of *it*, the wolf, devouring you). This is my wish for you as you face the challenge of making your dream of living abroad happen.

I hope I've inspired you to create such an adventure—because I know it will be a gift beyond measure, one that will make your world bigger, your empathy deeper, your understanding greater, and your family closer. A gift that doesn't stop giving.

I also know how easy it would have been *not* to do a year abroad. Fortunately, I had a partner who kept pushing the notion as a foregone conclusion (thank you, honey, for being you!). But left to my own devices, I very well might not have followed through.

When I was gathering stories for this book, I asked people who had done an adventure abroad to share their best tip for those who harbor the same dream. Carole Wells, who sailed around the globe with her family, shared words that spoke to me and I think will speak to you: "Go. Your boat will never be all ready. You will never have enough money. The world will never be at peace."

It's so ridiculously easy to succumb to the inertia that your boat is never ready, that you lack the funds, that the timing isn't right in the world.

And it's so easy for me to tell you to do it anyway.

But it's on you to slay the wolf.

ACKNOWLEDGMENTS

MANY THANKS TO EVERYONE who helped bring this book into being. I am grateful to those who shared the stories of their adventures: Le Billington and Jon Joseph; Stuart Brown and Michelle Radford-Brown; Tracey Carisch (traceycarisch.com); Michelle Damiani (MichelleDamiani.com); Lora Gordon; Stanley Holt and Jacqueline Bendy; Katy Mayo Hudson and David Hudson; Annette Jannotta (annettejannotta.com); John Kin and Frances Durcan; Laura Wall Mansfield (taproot. ventures); Rossella Mariotti-Jones and Moses Jones; Amy Maroney (amymaroney.com); George Mason and Salli Slaughter (worldhop.com and authorsroad.com); Andrea and Dan Pether; Rebecca Ponzi (fratelliponzi.com); Ryanne Rothenberg (rystable. com); Jen Shafer (SlowlyGlobal.blogspot.com); Erica Vaughn (mydoterra.com/ericavaughn); Jeremy and Christine Vyska (jeremy.vyska.info); Carole Wells (chasingsunsetsthebook.com);

Loey Werking Wells (pedestrianstories.com); Linda; and Stephen and Tanya. Thanks to all those who took the time to answer my questions.

With special thanks to Bridget and Kevin Kresse (kevinkresse. com), who inspired us and cheered us on as we dove into the deep end to make our year in Genoa happen.

To Alessandra Gardino (customizedjourneys.com), Sarah Richardson Green, Elizabeth Petrosian (lettersfromflorence.blogspot. com), and Helen Lenda and Hynek Chaloupka—I am so glad the stars aligned for us to know you! Thank you for being there.

Thank you to those who gave me feedback on early drafts, especially Megan Mahar Barnett and Hillary Tinapple.

And special thanks to all the *genovesi* who helped to make our year an unforgettable one, particularly Silvia Lacerra, Oscar Penniello, Tommy and Emanuele; Laura Ligabue, Nicola Grendi, and Caterina; Gabriella Tuccillo; and all the former 2M & 5M families at Scuola Mazzini.

ENDNOTES

1   If you're curious to learn about our experience as it unfolded, check out giorni-a-genova.blogspot.com. And in case you're wondering, we kept the lice out of it, though a couple of nits did make an appearance should you be game for a photo "treasure" hunt.

2   More than twenty families who have created an adventure abroad were surveyed for this book. I try to protect their privacy by not offering too many personal details. I also note where they have published about their experiences [see Appendix].

3   https://www.ted.com/talks/simon_sinek_how_great_leaders_inspire_action

4   https://www.psychologytoday.com/blog/ulterior-motives/200905/if-you-want-succeed-don-t-tell-anyone
http://www.psych.nyu.edu/gollwitzer/09_Gollwitzer_Sheeran_Seifert_Michalski_When_Intentions_.pdf

5   http://100waystochangetheworld.com/going-global-making-a-long-international-trip-happen-for-your-family/

6   Here are two articles: https://www.artsy.net/article/artsy-editorial-creative-work-vacation; https://michaelhyatt.com/the-science-of-sabbaticals/ Search sabbatical + creativity for plenty more.

7   https://statisticstimes.com/population/global-peace-index.php and the comprehensive report that links to it: http://visionofhumanity.org/indexes/global-peace-index/

8   A few top examples: transitionsabroad.com

Expatfocus.com

Expatexchange.com

9   Dan Clements and Tara Gignac, Escape 101, Sabbaticals Made Simple, p. 104.

10   https://www.ted.com/talks/stefan_sagmeister_the_power_of_time_off/transcript?language=en

11   Burkhard Bilger, "The Possibilian," The New Yorker, April 25, 2011.

12   A study at the University College of London looked at the brain functioning of taxi drivers, who memorize the city's labyrinthine streets over the course of their training. It turns out that the brain images before and after successful training show significant increase in the size of the hippocampus, or memory center. Not surprisingly, the trained cabbies outscored the control group in a variety of memory tests unrelated to the streets of London.

https://www.scientificamerican.com/article/london-taxi-memory/

13   Also in conjunction with the University College of London, this study measured activity in the area of the brain connected to motivation and reward. Subjects participated in a series of tests involving a variety of images, including those that were familiar, rare, negative, emotional, and completely novel. While connected to an MRI machine, the subjects' motivation

and reward center lit up more significantly when completely novel images popped up. Further, when these new and unexpected images were connected to a memory and recall test, the subjects performed better, suggesting that we learn better and more deeply when we are introduced to new stimuli.

http://www.scientificamerican.com/article/learning-by-surprise/

14   From: http://time.com/4721715/phenomena-annie-jacobsen/

"According to the Pentagon, the program was born of field reports from the war theater, including a 2006 incident in Iraq, when Staff Sergeant Martin Richburg, using intuition, prevented carnage in an IED, or improvised explosive device, incident. Commander Joseph Cohn, a program manager at the naval office, told the New York Times, 'These reports from the field often detailed a "sixth sense" or "Spidey sense" that alerted them to an impending attack or I.E.D., or that allowed them to respond to a novel situation without consciously analyzing the situation.'"

15   https://www.linkedin.com/pulse/wake-up-from-sleep-walking-through-life-rebecca-ponzi (August 12, 2015)

APPENDIX

ADDITIONAL READING

Bernick, Elisa. 2007. *The Family Sabbatical Handbook: The Budget Guide to Living Abroad with Your Family.* Branford, CT: Intrepid Traveler.

Carisch, Tracey. 2018. *Excess Baggage: One Family's Around-the-World Search for Balance.* Berkeley, CA: She Writes Press.

Clements, Dan, and Tara Gignac. 2007. *Escape 101: The Four Secrets to Taking a Career Break without Losing Your Money or Your Mind.* Creemore, Ont.: Brain Ranch.

Damiani, Michelle. 2015. *Il Bel Centro: A Year in the Beautiful Center.* Charlottesville, VA: Rialto Press.

Frost, Maya. 2009. *The New Global Student: Skip the SAT, Save Thousands on Tuition, and Get a Truly International Education.* New York: Three Rivers Press.

Guillebeau, Chris. 2017. *Side Hustle: From Idea to Income in 27 Days.* New York: Crown Business.

Kiyosaki, Robert T. 2017. *Rich Dad, Poor Dad: What the Rich Teach Their Kids about Money—That the Poor and Middle*

Class Do Not! Scottsdale, AZ: Plata Publishing.

Pane, Lawrence, Carole Wells Pane, and Ryan Pane. 2005. *Chasing Sunsets: A Practicing Devout Coward's Circumnavigation with His Wife and Son.* Burbank, CA: Raymond Hill Publishing.

Westphal, Chris. 2001. *A Family Year Abroad: How to Live Outside the Borders.* Scottsdale, AZ: Great Potential Press.

GENERAL RESEARCH AND FINDING AMBASSADORS

Anywhereist.com

Expatexchange.com

Expatfocus.com

Expatforum.com

Transitionsabroad.com

Search expat + forum + [target country] for others

SAMPLE CHECKLIST FROM AUTHOR'S FAMILY YEAR ABROAD

OBTAIN VISA FOR ITALY

- ☐ Complete Long Term Visa Application Form
- ☐ Visa Fee—get money order or cashier's check payable to the Consulate General of Italy (no cash, no credit cards, no personal checks)
- ☐ Get recent passport style photo following guidelines
- ☐ Ensure US passports are valid 3 months beyond planned stay *and* photocopy
- ☐ Get girls' birth certificates notarized with parents' authorization & ID
- ☐ Obtain copy of marriage certificate, after confirming if needed
- ☐ Documented and detailed guarantee of income (Copy of account statements for 6 months, rental agreement for our house, letters of good standing from bank, proof of financial assets to satisfy Italian authorities)
- ☐ Rental agreement for place in Italy
- ☐ Make flight reservations
- ☐ Find valid foreign medical insurance and get a declaration from the insurer stating that we are covered abroad
- ☐ FBI criminal report for adults (a report provided by an FBI approved channeler is sufficient)
- ☐ Write applicant letter that specifies the reason for our stay in Italy, length of stay and where we plan to reside, name of family members on visa application

PRACTICAL LIFE PREP FOR ITALY
Electronics misc.

- ☐ GPS with current Europe maps
- ☐ Adaptors for Europe/Italy

Prescriptions/Rx (list)

- ☐ Rx 1
- ☐ Rx 2
- ☐ Supplement 1

Mail and Phone Forwarding

- ☐ Suspend/transfer magazine subscriptions (list)
- ☐ Fill out USPS forms for mail forwarding
- ☐ Note in calendar to extend mail forwarding if needed
- ☐ Suspend phones/numbers here
- ☐ Research phone options in Italy
- ☐ Ensure cellphones are SIM-enabled to use in Italy

Packing – Key Decisions/Items

- ☐ Figure out what to ship to Italy in advance
- ☐ Determine any tax docs we'll need for next year
- ☐ Get initial Euros
- ☐ Get PIN for credit card or chip & pin card to use overseas

Contact Italy Connections

- ☐ Letter to teachers at girls' school in Genoa
- ☐ Make contact with cousins and other "ambassadors" (list)

PREP HOUSE FOR RENTERS

- ☐ Get plastic bins for storage

- ☐ Set up one room to lock up with valuable/personal items
- ☐ Living room

  - ○ Items to fix
  - ○ Items to cull/donate

- ☐ Dining Room

  - ○ Make note for renters about where things are
  - ○ Items to cull/donate
  - ○ Items to fix
  - ○ Transfer valuable items to attic

- ☐ Kitchen

  - ○ Items that need repair
  - ○ Cull useless items and donate extra cookbooks
  - ○ Make note for renters about where things are, directions for use, etc.

- ☐ Basement

  - ○ Items to cull/donate
  - ○ Items to fix
  - ○ Personal items to transfer to attic
  - ○ Note/label emergency food supply, etc.

- ☐ Master Bedroom

  - ○ Empty out drawers and closet
  - ○ Decide what to bring, what to store, what to donate

☐ Chiara Bedroom

    ○ Decide what to bring, what to store, what to donate
    ○ Thin out books and toys (keep some for renters)
    ○ Note sleeping bags & extra blankets in closet
    ○ Note soccer supplies in closet

☐ Mattea Bedroom

    ○ Decide what to bring, what to store, what to donate
    ○ Thin out books and toys (leave appropriate ones for renters)

☐ Organize big donations
☐ Recharge fire extinguishers
☐ Get 1–2 more CO_2 detectors
☐ Make list of house quirks
☐ Cancel service providers (list)
☐ Sell car
☐ Banking & bills

    ○ Go paperless
    ○ Set up wire payments
    ○ Inform Credit Card companies of foreign travel
    ○ Prepay some bills (e.g. life insurance)

WRAP UP

☐ School

    ○ Donate fish (and what else?) to school.

☐ Backup computers

    ○ Disk/thumb drive safekeeping?

☐ Personal

    ○ Put health records on USB drive to bring
    ○ Get annual checkups (incl. eye and dental) and make sure vaccinations are up-to-date
    ○ Get copy of vaccination record

☐ Practice Italian!

ABOUT THE AUTHOR

JACQUELINE JANNOTTA IS A writer, mom, informed educator, experienced traveler, and eternal optimist who inspires others to break free from the ordinary.

Her own career path has been anything but conventional, beginning with her work in television for entertainment industry giants like Warner Bros and Walt Disney. She went on to develop and write content for trailblazing internet firms, and founded ScoopOnSchools.com: helping parents navigate and expand the educational possibilities for their children.

It's in this spirit that Jacqueline organized her family's extraordinary year abroad in Genoa, Italy, captured in *Let's Leave the Country!* Inside these pages, Jacqueline has created the definitive guidebook she wished she'd had when embarking on her family's adventure.

Today, she lives with her husband and two daughters in Portland, Oregon, where she invites others to steward a better world at BecomingBetterPeople.us.

About the Interior Artist

MATTEA ROTHENBERG IS THE author's 12-year-old daughter and an avid sketch artist. Her family's year in Italy inspired and motivated Mattea to craft the hand-drawn illustrations seen at the head of each chapter in *Let's Leave the Country!*

Made in the USA
Middletown, DE
19 November 2022

15524636R00136